Marcellus Laroon

Marcellus Laroon

ROBERT RAINES

The Paul Mellon Foundation for British Art 1966

London Routledge & Kegan Paul

New York Pantheon Books

First published in Great Britain 1967
by The Paul Mellon Foundation for British Art, 38 Bury Street,
London, S.W.1 in association with Routledge & Kegan Paul Ltd.,
Broadway House, Carter Lane, London, E.C.4 and with
Pantheon Books, New York, N.Y., a Division of
Random House, Inc.

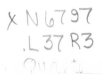
Library of Congress catalogue card no. 67–16158
Printed in Great Britain by Westerham Press, Westerham, Kent
Designed in the offices of The Paul Mellon
Foundation for British Art

Contents

Photographic Acknowledgements

Ashmolean Museum, Oxford Figs 35, 40, 46, 67; Pls 12, 66, 67, 68. Bath Academy of Art Fig 63. Birmingham City Art Gallery Pl 23. Museum Boymans van Beunengen, Rotterdam Fig 48. British Museum Figs 18, 41, 42, 43, 47, 53, 64, 68; Pls 15, 24, 25, 40. A. C. Cooper Ltd, London Figs 17, 36; Pls 21, 30, 31, 42, 51, 52, 63, 65. Courtauld Institute of Art, University of London Figs 16, 50, 52, 58, 69; Pls 6, 11, 22, 38, 43, 71, 72. Fitzwilliam Museum, Cambridge Figs 11, 22, 55. R. B. Fleming & Co *The Cryes of the City of London* pp19–39; Pls 5, 26. Fodor Collection, Amsterdam Fig 21. John R. Freeman & Co, London Figs 59, 60, 61, 66; Pls 39, 50, 57. E. & D. Gibbs, London Fig 5; Pl 35. Hornby Autograph Collection, Liverpool Fig 1. Huntington Library & Art Gallery, California Pls 14, 18. Minneapolis Institute of Arts Fig 39. National Gallery of Ireland, Dublin Fig 25c, 37. Magdalene College, Cambridge Figs 9, 10. Photo Studios, London Pl 58. Tom Scott, Edinburgh Fig 38; Pl 8. Service de Documentation Photographique Réunion des Musées Nationaux, France Fig 34. Tate Gallery, London Fig 25b; Pls 45, 73. Whitworth Art Gallery, Manchester Pl 13. City Art Gallery, York Pl 44.

List of Illustrations

Foreword

It is difficult in a study which has been in slow progress for many years to mention individually all those who have helped in one way or another but I hope that omission will not be taken to imply ingratitude. I am indeed grateful to all those who have answered my enquiries, who have sent information unasked and without whose help this book would have been much less complete than it is. Anyone working on lesser-known English painters must very soon be aware that without the Walpole Society's meticulous edition of Vertue's notebooks and the Witt library of photographs his task would be immeasurably more difficult. It is then perhaps not inappropriate to acknowledge first the great value of these two sources.

I am especially indebted to Sir Osbert Sitwell, Mr R. E. Alton, Mr A. W. Aspital, Mr E. Croft-Murray, and Mr L. G. Duke; to Dr S. G. Gudlaugsson who has sent me information about works by Laroon in continental sales; to Professor Alastair Smart, then of Hull University, for his advice and encouragement in the earlier stages of this study, and to Dr Malcolm Easton and Mr Oliver Millar who have read and advised on the manuscript; to Mr Sidney Sabin and Mr William Drummond of the Sabin Galleries; and to my wife whose knowledge of painting and of historical costume and whose keen eye on the manuscript in all its stages have been a constant help.

I am no less indebted to the officials and members of the staffs of many galleries, libraries and museums, especially the British Museum, the Victoria and Albert Museum, the National Portrait Gallery, the Pepysian Library at Magdalene College, Cambridge, the Guildhall Library, the Courtauld Institute of Art and the Society for Army Historical Research; to Messrs Christie, Manson and Woods Ltd who allowed me access to their archives, to Messrs Sotheby and Co. and the many dealers who have searched their records and who have sent me much invaluable information.

I wish to express my gratitude to Her Majesty the Queen for gracious permission to reproduce works in the Royal Collection, to Her Royal Highness Princess Marina, Duchess of Kent, for kind permission to reproduce the painting in her possession, and to all those owners who have allowed me to see and to reproduce their pictures and who have supplied information and often photographs.

Finally I wish to thank the Paul Mellon Foundation for British Art for making it possible to publish and to illustrate so fully this work on a British painter and to thank the staff, especially Mr Kenneth Sharpe and Mr Dudley Snelgrove, for unfailing kindness and co-operation; and to express the deepest gratitude to the Director of the Foundation, Mr Basil Taylor, whose advice and comments over several years have given me new ideas or caused me to reconsider old ones and whose detailed suggestions after his editorial reading have been immensely valuable.

R.R.

Introduction

Captain Marcellus Laroon, whose life and work is the main subject of this study, was musician, singer, professional soldier and man of pleasure, who drew and painted, 'for diversitions' as Vertue puts it, from childhood until the year of his death at the age of ninety-three. He has been referred to as 'an interesting mannerist', as an 'imitator of Hogarth' and as 'an amateur of the calibre of Constantin Guys'. Sir Osbert Sitwell, always his admirer, has likened him in his career and in the artistic interest he showed in the life around him, to Sickert, who, Sir Osbert tells us, was himself fascinated by Laroon's work. [1]

Since Randall Davies remarked in 1907 that three or four drawings, 'quite as skilful and nearly as elegant as Gravelot', and the two paintings at Kensington Palace were all that he had seen, [2] much of his work has come to light, and is still appearing. In 1931 Tancred Borenius expressed surprise that no monograph had been written on this 'artist of singular fascination' whose champion he had himself wished to become; [3] in 1935 Ralph Edwards wrote on the conversation pieces; [4] in the following year Sacheverell Sitwell devoted several pages and a number of plates to him; [5] and in 1959 the present writer published a catalogue of Laroon's work as far as it was known to him at that time. [6]

Born in 1679 Laroon was the son and grandson of painters of similar name and the attempt must therefore be immediately made to clarify their relationship and to establish the nomenclature which may save the reader from confusion. Laroon is the anglicised version of the surname Lauron used, except occasionally, by the father. Until very recently it was thought that the original family name might have been Laurens, the spelling on two drawings tentatively attributed to the grandfather, but it now seems unlikely that this draughtsman, who signs *M aurens*, had any connection with the Lauron family. Hereafter Lauron will be used for the father who in earlier literature was often called Old Laroon, and Laroon for the artist who is the chief subject of this book and who has been frequently referred to as Captain Laroon or Laroon the Younger. [7]

Unlike his father, Laroon painted mainly for his own pleasure and seems, after retirement from the Army in 1732, to have had money enough to support a comfortable bachelor life without need to have practised in those pictorial forms which would in the eighteenth century have ensured a livelihood. The combined working lives of Lauron and Laroon spanned about a century from the former's admission to the Painter-Stainers' Company in 1674 to 1772 the date of his son's last drawings.

1 O. Sitwell, *Noble Essences*, 1950, pp199, 202–3.

2 R. Davies, *English Society of the Eighteenth Century in Contemporary Art*, 1907, p34.

3 T. Borenius, 'The Kaleidoscope of Taste', *The Studio*, December, 1931, pp352–63.
4 R. Edwards, 'The Conversation Pictures of Marcellus Laroon', *Apollo*, October, 1935, pp193–8.
5 S. Sitwell, *Conversation Pieces*, 1936, pp71–3.
6 R. Raines, 'Marcellus Laroon the Younger – II', *Connoisseur Year Book*, 1959, pp113–22.

7 It should be noted that in Croft-Murray and Hulton's *Catalogue of British Drawings* (British Museum), vol. I (1960) 'Marcellus I Laroon' refers to the grandfather, 'Marcellus II' to Lauron, and 'Marcellus III' to Laroon. Confusion has existed between Laroon and his brother John, also painter and musician. Their names have frequently been combined and paintings and drawings attributed to John Marcellus Laroon (see pp43–45). For further notes about the family see Appendix I.

In this study an attempt is made to tell the story of Laroon's life, to comment on his work and his relations with his contemporaries, and to catalogue his paintings and drawings as completely as present knowledge will allow. The work of his father, whose employment as studio assistant, and whose versatility as painter, miniaturist, engraver and draughtsman, probably exemplify the life of the lesser but successful craftsman at the end of the seventeenth century, is briefly described.

The two main sources of information about Laroon are the brief autobiographical sketch printed by John Thomas Smith in *Nollekens and his Times*,[1] and the scattered references in Vertue's notebooks. Laroon's clear and succinct but impersonal and incomplete account of his life, of which the manuscript is lost, occupies ten of Smith's pages – about 3000 words. It opens with a short account of his family and his youth, continues with his army experiences and closes with his final retirement from the army in 1732. With anyone as unreliable as John Thomas Smith, who was certainly not above embroidering a good story to make it better and probably of inventing one if need be, it is important to examine critically not only what he writes but what he quotes. There are a number of mistakes in proper and place names, which I have checked with Army records; and some points of confusion in the accounts of battles – particularly of Balaquer and Almenara. On the whole I am inclined to think that it is a reasonably reliable transcript of a manuscript, written by Laroon soon after his retirement from the Army in 1732, and that omissions and major errors in dates are the result of his own failure of memory, while minor errors may be attributed to Smith's inaccuracy. Smith's other comments on Laroon which will be mentioned from time to time are usually questionable, and little is added to our knowledge by this sort of remark: 'His (Laroon's) family were frequently mentioned by Mr Nollekens, as one of the most eccentric with whom his father and mother had been intimate'.

As Vertue, who has some twenty notes (a few of them fairly long ones) on Lauron and Laroon, makes his final entry in 1742, knowledge of the last thirty years of the life of the latter is meagre. I have attempted however to reconstruct from him, from Smith and from other sources a consecutive story. I am well aware that Laroon's Army career has little place in what is intended to be primarily an art-historical study; especially as his military adventures appear to have provided him with so few subjects. Even this is perhaps of value if it reminds us of the often tenuous connection between some aspects of a painter's life and his art; and it seems unreasonable to leave out an activity which occupied the greater part of twenty-five years of the life of one's subject.

1 J. T. Smith, *Nollekens and his Times*, 1829, vol. II, pp255–74; ed. W. Whitten, 1920, vol. II, pp190–205. Quotations not identified by footnotes are from Laroon's autobiography as printed by Smith, but with the correction of some proper and place names.

Fig 1 William Humphrey *Marcellus Lauron* engraving

Marcellus Lauron[1]

1 For the distinction between Lauron and Laroon see page 2.

Sometime before the middle of the seventeenth century the Frenchman, Marcel Lauron, had settled in the Hague where he married and where his wife, whose name and nationality are unknown, bore him a number of children. The second son of this marriage was the Marcellus Lauron who came when young to England, accompanied, according to some accounts, by his father. The date of his birth and of his arrival in this country remain uncertain: his son, Marcellus Laroon, writes that he came 'when a young man'; Buckeridge that 'being very young he came over with his father'.[2] A further complication arises from Vertue's somewhat contradictory accounts, in the 1713 notebook and the transcript, of Lauron's acquaintance with Rembrandt in York, during the latter's supposed visit to England.[3] Had this taken place even as late as 1661 as implied by Vertue in the notebook, Lauron would have been at the most only twelve years old, hardly a young man; but there seems no more valid reason for this date for Rembrandt's visit than for any other, either earlier or later. Vertue's accounts are not only contradictory but at least second-hand, his informant being Charles Christian Reisen, who may himself have been pretty unreliable, Vertue having described him as 'a Man of a Sarcastical humour [who] highly pleasd with his Oddities most of his companions'.

Much of Lauron's work is so essentially Dutch in subject and style, and his technique in mezzotints so much more akin to the rougher surface quality of the Dutch workers than to the smoother finish of the English, that apprenticeship in Holland seems inevitable.

Vertue continues that Lauron lived in Yorkshire for several years and 'the Countrys aboutt' and this statement, with the addition that he painted portraits there, has been repeated in nearly all references. No attributable portraits in or connected with Yorkshire have come to light, but this is no real argument against Lauron having resided in the county. A comparable, but rather later painter, James Parmentier, who is known to have lived in Yorkshire for some twenty years, told Vertue that he had earned more than three hundred pounds in one year by portraiture;[4] but only two certain Yorkshire portraits by him are known.[5] Lauron has, at any rate, left no early tracks in Yorkshire nor, indeed, has Rembrandt.

There is no doubt however that Lauron had later associations with the county, in particular with members of Ralph Thoresby's York-Leeds circle of virtuosi. In a letter of 15th July, 1682, James Smith, writing to his uncle Henry Gyles, the glass painter in York, refers to some pictures which 'Mr Lorowne' had begun.[6] Another

2 B. Buckeridge, *An Essay Towards an English School of Painters*, appended to R. de Piles, *The Art of Painting*, 2nd edition, 1744, p396, states that he was born in 1653 and that he died aged about fifty-two; Laroon that he died aged fifty-three. He is known to have died on 11th March 1701/2, *Marcelius Laroon of par. St Pauls (Covent) Gardeing, paintre*, so it is probable that he was born in 1648 or 9.

3 See Appendix II.

4 Walpole Society, *Vertue III*, p45.

5 The *Ralph Thoresby* in the collection of Sir Richard Sykes at Sledmere, and the signed and dated *Marmaduke Fothergill* of 1717, in the York Minster Library.

6 British Museum, Stowe MS. 746. f.57, printed in Knowles, 'Henry Gyles, the Glass Painter of York', *Walpole Society*. vol. XI, p66.

1 British Museum, Stowe MS. 746.f.60, printed *ibid*. pp65–6.

2 Court Minutes of the Painter Stainers' Company, Guildhall MS. 5667/2, 15th July, 1674.

3 The date of the marriage has not been found as the registers of Chiswick Parish, where it was probably solemnised, do not begin until 1678. Jeremiah Keene appears in the Church-wardens' Accounts during the years 1670 to 1686. He was buried on 14th March, 1693. The date of Laroon's birth is given according to his own statement, the records of his and his elder brother's births not having been found. Some information about other members of the family will be found in Appendix I.
4 Westminster Library, the Rate Books of St Paul's, Covent Garden. The house was assessed at 10s in 1680 and at 16s 8d in 1700. The assessment for Aid to the Crown (Corporation of London Records Office) in 1693/4, gives the annual rental assessment as £50, the tax being £10.
5 J. Stow, ed. J. Strype, *A Survey of the Cities of London and Westminster* – – – –, 1720, book VI. p87 et seq.

6 'a Fryers civil Chastisement by Larroon' was lot 113 in the sale of paintings at Will's on 18th November 1691 (British Museum Library, CUP. 645.e.5).

letter, written probably later in the same year, is not complimentary: 'As to Mr Lorowne I cannot gitt the picters of him and in truth the copy he has done I would not give him sixpence for it'. [1] A third letter, quoted later, refers to other paintings.

Lauron was certainly in London by 1674 when, on 15th July, he appeared at the Painter-Stainers' Company 'and paid his Quarteridge And promised to bring his proofe peece'. [2] About this date, or perhaps rather later, he married Elizabeth Keene, daughter of Jeremiah Keene, a builder of Little Sutton near Chiswick. Keene was a man of some position and responsibility, churchwarden and church councillor, who seems to have achieved, in that earlier period of speculative building, the not unusual transition from craftsman to employer. [3] Two sons were born, John on a date unknown and Marcellus on 2nd April, 1679, before Lauron took possession, at midsummer quarterday 1680, of the house on the west side of Bow Street where he was to live for the rest of his life. [4] Bow Street, 'open and large, with very good Houses, well inhabited, and resorted unto by Gentry for Lodgings', [5] ran parallel to the east side of the Piazza of Covent Garden, extending from Russell Street on the south to end in New Broad Court on the north. Covent Garden had for some twenty years been one of the fashionable areas of London, and as late as 1720 Strype, in *A Survey of the Cities of London and Westminster*, was still able to write:

'If we consider this Parish, as to its fine, straight and broad Streets, replenished with such good Buildings, and so well inhabited by a Mixture of Nobility, Gentry, and wealthy Tradesmen, here seated since the Fire of London 1666, scarce admitting of any Poor, not being pestered with mean Courts and Alleys; likewise its open and large Piazza or Garden, so delightful to walk in: It may deservedly be reckoned one of the best Parishes in the Cities of *London* and *Westminster*, or Parts adjacent'. [5]

But contemporary records of vice and immorality, centred especially in the Piazza, suggest that Strype is giving only one side of the picture.

Nothing certain is known of Lauron's work before his arrival in Bow Street. It remains conjectural how he could so soon afford to take a good house in a fashionable street where the other residents included such successful people as Grinling Gibbons, who owned a painting by him, Thomas Jordan the poet, who amongst many City activities devised a number of Lord Mayor's Shows, William Longueville the wealthy lawyer and Dr Richard Lower 'the most noted physician in Westminster and London'. His early biographers insist that his forte was copying – Horace Walpole reporting that his father 'had a picture by him that easily passed for Bassan's' – and an able copyist could expect a reasonable if not a generous return for his work. He may already have been assisting Kneller, who moved a year later to the north-east corner of the Piazza, and whose success, as early as this, could have imposed the need for assistance. He may perhaps have worked for other painters and a possible association with Antonio Verrio will be considered later. For the sale of his own work the proximity of Will's Coffee House, next door but two, would have been useful as coffee houses were often the site for auction sales: one painting by Lauron, *A Fryer's civil Chastisement*, is recorded as for sale there in 1691 but it seems likely that he would have made considerable use during his twenty years in Bow Street of such a convenient and popular meeting place. [6]

In these surroundings Lauron's children grew up; among the fashionable, the intelligent and the disreputable, with the intellectuals close by at Will's and the no doubt more interesting undesirables at Oxford Kate's, an unseemly tavern at the other end of Bow Street; a world of which the poorer and seamier characters were depicted in Lauron's engraved book *The Cryes of the City of London*.[1]

After the artist's removal to Bow Street, his wife, Elizabeth, who is mentioned neither in his will of 1701 nor in his son's memoir, had given birth to four more children two of whom survived: James born in 1684 and Elizabeth born in 1689. In his will Lauron left furniture and furnishings to his 'kinswoman' Mrs Elizabeth Burgess who perhaps filled the place at least of housekeeper after his wife's death.

Several self-portraits of Lauron are recorded but the only known representations are the engraving by William Humphrey, entitled *Laroon Drawing Master to King William the Third* [Fig 1]†, and an engraving in Dalloway's edition of Walpole's *Anecdotes*, with a note to the effect that 'the head here given is curious as hitherto there has been no engraving of him; it was copied from a miniature of the same size, many years since by Mr G. P. Harding'. Both prints were made many years after Lauron's death but may be authentic, the former showing him in early life and the latter, a crude cut, in middle age.[2]

Vertue's poor opinion of his character seems to have been based partly on the evidence of his works – 'his thoughts in his pictures shew him to be a Man of *levity*. of loose conversation & *morals* suteable to his birth & education. being *low & spurious*'.[3] and partly on information from Laroon who had recounted to Vertue one of his father's exploits – 'one night going homewards with some other companions. met & quarreld in the street. swords were drawn. Cut and wounded about the head & his nose & lip almost cutt off. he has painted his own picture where he has represented the scarrs, as it appeard afterwards'.[4] But whatever his personal pleasures may have been, his care of his sons' education was exemplary. Laroon writes:

'We were three sons left, brought up by him to painting, and my father gave us other necessary learning and accomplishments; we had French-masters, learned writing, arithmetic, fencing, and dancing. He entertained in his house a very good master of music, whose name was Moret, who performed on several instruments, – with design, as my father had a very good ear, to learn of him to play on the six-stringed viol; but my elder brother, ten years old, took up the instrument, and executing Moret's instructions better than my father, he ordered him to teach my brother. We had frequent concerts of music at our house. I was then about seven or eight years of age, and was judged to have an inclination to music, by being often found scraping on a fiddle in some private place. I was then put under Moret's discipline, to learn to play on the violin. We both made such progress, that in about two years we could perform *à livre ouvert*'.

During these years, Lauron's diverse activities, in addition to the task of teaching three sons his own art, must have kept him fully occupied and have provided him, not with a fortune, but at least with sufficient for his family needs. With little time probably to teach others than his own sons, he had, according to Buckeridge, one pupil – Thomas Pembroke, a history painter who died young about 1690, and if the inscription on the engraved portrait of Lauron, by William Humphrey, is to be credited he was drawing-master to King William. He is similarly described in the advertisement of Laroon's sale in 1775, when one lot was 'a striking Portrait of Old Laroon, Drawing Master to King William the Third by himself'. No documentary support has been found for this appointment.[5]

His main source of income was probably his employment in Kneller's studio. Usually described as a painter of draperies, his versatility would make him an invaluable assistant to the master. His painting of accessories, as in the portrait of Charles II [Fig 2], is thoroughly competent, and the existence of two flower pieces, not signed but attributed to him in an old inventory, suggests that he may have been

[1] See Appendix III for the *Cryes* and *The Art of Defence*.

† Figure references are to illustrations in the text and catalogue. Plate references are to illustrations in the sequence beginning on page 155.

[2] George Perfect Harding (1778 to 1853) made watercolour copies of many historical portraits. A volume in the Royal Library at Windsor contains twenty-one of these, mostly of the Stuart period. (see A. P. Oppé, *English Drawings at Windsor Castle*, nos. 310–314). William Humphrey (?1740 to ?1810) was a somewhat obscure engraver, who worked chiefly in mezzotint. Later in life he took to print selling and acted as agent for a number of collectors.
[3] Walpole Society, *Vertue I*, p147.
[4] *Ibid*. p122.

[5] Mr Oliver Millar has kindly informed me that he knows of no other indication, in the Royal Archives or elsewhere, that Lauron held this position.

Fig 2 Marcellus Lauron *Charles II* Oil on canvas approx. 180 inches high Christ's Hospital, Horsham

responsible for some of the flower painting in Kneller's portraits.[1]

Looking at the list of a dozen or so painters who seem at one time or another, to have worked for Kneller, it is difficult to see his studio as a very highly organised portrait factory, but rather as a somewhat loose congeries of assistants, pupils and later, members of the Kneller Academy. Assistants other than Lauron mentioned by Vertue are Jan Baptist Gaspars, known as 'Lely's Baptiste' from his work for that master, who later painted postures and draperies for Kneller; Jan Pieters III, who studied under Kneller for some years and worked for him for many, painting draperies; John James Backer who went with Kneller to Brussels to paint the equestrian portrait of Maximilian Emmanuel, Duke of Bavaria; and Edward Byng, who seems to have been a full-time assistant during Kneller's later years. In addition a 'Mr Weedman' and a 'Mr Swartz' are listed as 'painters to Sr. G. Kneller' by Vertue in his account of the opening of Kneller's Academy in 1711. Other painters appear to have been called in for occasional help; for instance, according to Pilkington, John Wyck painted the horse and the background battle in the equestrian portrait of Frederick, First Duke of Schomberg, although Elsum's epigram tells us that both horse and rider were 'by Appelles Hand'; and Henry Vergazoon, Walpole records, sometimes painted backgrounds.

The earliest known portrait by Lauron himself is the *Charles II* painted for the Mathematical School of Christ's Hospital [Fig 2]. It is the subject of a number of entries in the Court Minutes of the Hospital, which give not only an idea of Lauron's customary prices, but throw some light on the summary treatment that artists could receive from their patrons. The first minute on 19th June, 1684, of a recommendation from the Committee of the Schooles to the Court of Governors reads:

'The Committee doe agree if the Court shall thinke fitt to have the King's Majestys picture welldrawne upon cloth in a warrlike posture by a very good hand and to be Set up between the two windows at the upper end of the Mathematicall Schoole and in it to be Shippes and what also may describe Navigation'.

This recommendation was accepted and at a meeting of the Court on 13th October, 1684, it was resolved that:

'Whereas a Committee of the 19th of June 1684 Did agree to have his Majs. picture well drawne upon Cloth to be sett up at the upper end of the New Mathematicall Schoole Now to this Committee Mr. Morsellis Lorone Limner tendered the draught of a figure which was very well liked and approved off. His demand for doeing of the Same well, according to the said sketch was £50 afterwards £40 the house to find the frame.

The Committee told him that if he did well upon Ticking not Canvas according to the figure, they would give him £30, the which he said was but little, saying that if he did it he would doe it for his owne as well as the Hospital's credit they told him, that if he did, and they were well Satisfied he deserved more, they would recommend him to the Court to be further considered off.

He told them he did not know how to agree to their proposal. But he was resolved forthwith to proceed to the work and when finished he would leave himself to them for Satisfaction.

The Committee were well pleased and desired him that when he had drawne the Outlines of what he did intend He would shew the Same to Secretary Pepys and to Mr. Pagett the Mathematicall Schoole Master, and when the Outlines were agreed to, then to finish the Same with all convenient speed'.

Four months later on 24th February, 1684/5 the Court received a report from the Committee to the effect that:

'At a Committee in Christ's Hospitall 24 Jany 1684. The said persons having received and considered of the picture drawne by Mr. Lauron in the Mathematicall Schoole agreed to allow him twenty four pounds and one Guinney to buy him a paire of Globes in full payment for the said picture which the

[1] As by *Lauroon* in a list of his paintings written by the ninth Earl of Exeter, (1725–1793), but in other catalogues as by Baptist, i.e. Baptiste Monnoyer.

Fig 3 Marcellus Lauron *John,
3rd Lord Lovelace* Oil on canvas
approx. 96 inches high
Wadham College, Oxford

1 C. H. Collins Baker, 'Antonio Verrio and
Thornhill's early Portraiture', *Connoisseur*,
March 1953, p12.
2 E. Croft-Murray, *Decorative Painting in
England*, vol. 1, 1963, p61.

3 It is suggested by E. Croft-Murray and
P. Hulton (*Catalogue of British Drawings in the
British Museum*, vol. I, 1960, p403) that this is
the engraving by Samuel Moore (British
Museum Print Room 1934–2–17–76). The
drawing for this print, which is not a processional picture but is of groups of figures in
processional order, may well have been by
Lauron, some of the figures being quite close
to his style.
4 William Savery, of Slade in Cornwood, was
the son of another William Savery and died in
1696, within two years of his father's death.
The portrait of Catherine Savery, also at
Plymouth, attributed to Lauron, is not by him.
5 Walpole Society, *Vertue IV*, p51.
6 *Ibid.* p165.
7 *Ibid.* p147.
8 The self-portraits which Vertue records are
one in the possession of John Laroon and a
copy at 'Mr. Bowkers the Chacer', two small
oils in the possession of Laroon (*Vertue I*,
p36), and one with scars received in a street
fight (*Vertue I*, p122).
9 In Coxe Macro's account book (Bodleian
English Miscellany, e.346, f.259), 'Old
Heemskirk's head by Old Larroon'.
10 Walpole Society, *Vertue I*, p147.

said Mr. Lauron accepted off and received his money accordingly.

The Court was well Satisfied therewith'.

We wonder if the painter was equally well satisfied when, two months later, he received his much diminished fee. Nevertheless comparison with the £300 which Verrio was paid by the Hospital for the vast painting, with a hundred or more figures, of James II receiving the mathematical scholars, suggests that Lauron was not so much underpaid.

There can be little if any doubt that the portrait to which these minutes refer is the one which now hangs in the library of Christ's Hospital at Horsham. A big canvas, some fifteen feet by ten, it shows the King, in an imperious if not a warlike posture, with a cannon and navigational instruments – globe, sextant and dividers – in the foreground, and ships, seen through a window, in the background. Collins Baker, who attributed it to Antonio Verrio because of stylistic affinities to the James II group, describes it as 'a grandiose full-length of Charles II' of heroic design 'with Venetian opulence and swagger'.[1] It is difficult to disagree either with this descrip-tion or with the stylistic association with the Verrio group, especially in the drapery painting. The group however provides its own problems, as it seems that Verrio was assisted by Louis Laguerre, Croft-Murray pointing out that Vertue's statement that Laguerre assisted Verrio at St Bartholomew's Hospital must have been a slip of the pen for Christ's Hospital, as there is nothing by either artist at St Bartholomew's.[2] The work of the two painters in the group has not been disentangled, and so it is difficult to say whose style of drapery painting Lauron's approaches. As far as Lauron is concerned there seem to be two possibilities: that he himself was responsible for some of the drapery work in the group, or that, as an experienced copyist, he adapted his style, for this commission, to conform with that of the group.

Whatever the solution of this particular problem the portrait establishes Lauron as an able painter of the formal portrait in the baroque tradition. The portrait of Lord Lovelace in peer's robes [Fig 3], which hangs in the Gallery of Wadham College, Oxford, is conventionally posed and less vigorous. It is inscribed:

John Lord Lovelace, . . . Capt of ye Band of Gent Pensioners to King William ye third, who came into England on ye fifth day of Novembr 1688, to redeem this Nation from Popery and Slavery.

This inscription and Lauron's engraving of the coronation procession[3] were intended no doubt to draw the new King's attention to a loyal Dutchman. Lauron's only other known portrait is the signed and dated *William Savery of Slade*, of 1690 [Fig 4], in the Cottonian Collection at Plymouth. With the face and hands well and delicately modelled and the draperies broadly and effectively handled, it is a sur-prisingly intimate portrait with considerable sensitivity to the sitter's personality, very different from his formal full-lengths.[4] Portraits of *John Bancroft*, the dramatist and surgeon,[5] *Caius Gabriel Cibber*, the sculptor[6] 'a head in his own hair, holding a small medalion in his hand – a ruff countenance – tho well painted', and somewhat ambiguously, *Mr Skinner*, the grandfather of 'Mr Skinner (who) keeps the George at Hatfield 1738',[7] and several self-portraits are mentioned by Vertue.[8] None of these has been identified, nor has the portrait of *Egbert van Heemskerck* from the collection of Dr Coxe Macro.[9]

Vertue asserts that Lauron's 'essays in face painting in small. & history had no great Success'.[10] His skill in 'face painting in small' can be judged only from a copy

Fig 5 Marcellus Lauron after
Lawrence Crosse
Duke of Monmouth
$3\frac{5}{16} \times 2\frac{13}{16}$ inches (oval)
Collection unknown

Fig 4 Marcellus Lauron *William Savery* Oil on canvas 30 × 25 inches
Cottonian Collection, City Art Gallery, Plymouth

[Fig 5] initialled *ML* and so presumably by Lauron, of a miniature of the
Duke of Monmouth painted by Lawrence Crosse in 1683.[1] A competent work, in
a style very like Crosse's own, it may have been a commissioned copy or perhaps
was done for practice. It bears out the general view of Lauron's abilities as a copyist,
at least as far as miniatures are concerned. A few history paintings are known to
have existed, an *Abraham offering up his son Isaac*, for instance, in Samuel Scott's sale,[2]
but all seem to have disappeared. They can now be judged only from engravings,

1 Exhibited Blairman's, 1951, but not in the
catalogue; sold at Christie's, 9th February
1960, (175).

2 Sale of Samuel Scott's paintings, 4th April,
1765, (62).

11

Fig 6 Marcellus Lauron *A Kestrel* Oil on paper on panel 12 9/16 × 7 7/8 inches Michael Bevan

and there is no evidence in the print of *Perseus and Andromeda* that Vertue's verdict was wrong, or that Lauron differed in any way from his many colleagues who had also failed in a genre to which the English artistic climate seems inimical.

Another activity may have been the insertion of staffage figures or animals in landscapes by other painters. A sale catalogue of 1713 lists 'A large Stag-Hunting by Lauron and Vandest'.[1] Vandest is presumably Adriaen van Diest, a painter of decorative landscapes, who worked in England from about 1678 until his death in 1704; and possibly Lauron painted the figures and animals for him. It has been said that the figures in some of van Diest's landscapes were by Adam Colonia,[2] but apart from this I know of no other suggestion that they were not his own: a signed and dated watercolour, of 1685, in the Cottonian Collection, shows him as very well able to do without such assistance.[3] Lauron's many figure drawings establish him however as a competent performer, while drawings of horses and two small paintings of a kestrel [Fig 6] and a spaniel, inscribed in an old hand *Painted by Old Laroon about the year 1670*, speak equally for him as an animal painter.[4]

1 *A Catalogue of extraordinary original Pictures at the Rainbow and Dove near Durham Yard*, 8th May, 1713, (5). (British Museum Library, C–M.534).

2 E. K. Waterhouse, *Painting in Britain, 1530–1790*, 1953, p113.

3 For van Diest, many of whose landscapes have small figures, see E. Croft-Murray and P. Hulton, *Catalogue of British Drawings*, pp534–5, and O. Millar, *Tudor, Stuart and Early Georgian Pictures in the Royal Collection*, 1963, p158, pl.160. He is often described as a landscape and portrait painter but I think there is some confusion with a later 'Mr Vandest – face painter' who was visited in Newport Street by the Earl of Egmont in 1732 (*Hist. MSS. Comm. Egmont*, vol. I, p257), and who was presumably the G. van Diest who signed and dated a portrait of the sixth Viscount Montagu in 1736, recorded by Duleep Singh, *Portraits in Norfolk Houses*, 1927, vol. II, p116, as then at Oxburgh Hall.
4 *A Spaniel*, oil on canvas on panel, 8 9/16 x 6in. and *A Kestrel*, oil on paper on panel, 12 9/16 x 7 7/8 in. They were lot 121 at Sotheby's, 31st January, 1951; then with Spink and Son, from where the latter passed into the collection of the late Captain Richard Briscoe and then into that of Mr Michael Bevan.

Fig 7 Marcellus Lauron *Buy my fat chickens* (drawing for *The Cryes of London*) Pen and grey wash over pencil 8 7/16 × 6 1/8 inches R. E. Alton

Fig 8 Marcellus Lauron *Six pence a pound fair Cherryes* (drawing for *The Cryes of London*) Pen and grey wash over pencil 8 7/16 × 6 1/8 inches R. E. Alton

5 Both pen and grey wash over pencil, indented for transfer, 8 7/16 x 6 1/8 in. in the collection of Mr R. E. Alton, Oxford.
6 These are two of twelve drawings which can confidently be assigned to Lauron, in Pepys MS. 2973 in the Pepysian Library at Magdalene College, Cambridge, *My Collection of Prints & Drawings relating to London & Westminster etc. – Put together Anno Domini 1700*. See R. Raines, 'Drawings by Marcellus Lauron – 'Old Laroon' – in the Pepysian Library', *Apollo*, May 1965, 'Notes on British Art', where the drawings are listed and five are reproduced.
7 Nine in the Witt Collection, Courtauld Institute, one in the Fitzwilliam Museum, one in the writer's possession and three (1965) at the Sabin Galleries.
8 For plate 8 'The Sword and Dagger Guard: The Sword that offers first is Defended by ye Dagger'; in the Print Room of the British Museum. See also Appendix III.

Two drawings for plates for *The Cryes of London*, *Buy my fat chickens* and *Six pence a pound fair cherryes*[5] [Figs 7,8], a number of drawings in the Pepysian Library, of which two are here reproduced, *The Sheriff and his Officers* and *An Execution at Tyburn*[6] [Figs 9,10], some small drawings on the backs of roughly made playing cards [Fig 11],[7] and the drawing for a plate for *The Art of Defence* [Fig 12][8] all show Lauron to have been a skilful, accomplished and vigorous draughtsman, in spite of occasional faults in anatomy and perspective and an exaggerated contraposto especially evident

6.

Fig 9 Marcellus Lauron *The Sheriff and his Officers* Pencil and brown wash 7⅞ × 10 inches
Pepysian Library, Magdalene College, Cambridge

1 Two in the British Museum (E. Croft-Murray and P. Hulton, *Catalogue of British Drawings*, p404, pls.197 and 8) and one in the collection of Mr and Mrs Paul Mellon.

2 F. Antal, *Hogarth and his place in European Art*, 1962, p230, n.88.

3 See Appendix III for *The Cryes* and *The Art of Defence*.

in walking figures. He drew also several fencing scenes in black chalk[1] which were not used for but are closely related to *The Art of Defence*. The plates in this book are, on the whole, less well engraved than those in *The Cryes of London* and do little justice to Lauron's draughtsmanship.

The *Cryes* have been described by Antal as being in a 'moderate baroque' style.[2] If one accepts Antal's inclusive use of the term 'baroque', then this is true, but only of some plates. Nothing could be much less baroque than for instance *The London Quaker, Buy any Wax or Wafers* or *Any Card matches* or *Savealls*, which are flat, linear and far from painterly. What is remarkable about so many is their realism – *Ha Ha Ha Poor Jack, The London Begger, Four for Six pence Mackrell* or *Twelve Pence a Peck Oysters* – with only an occasional touch of caricature or satire. The plates vary widely in quality and many give no hint of the spontaneity of the drawings, if one can judge from the two already mentioned, especially that for *Cherryes* which has something of the feeling of Hogarth's *Shrimp Girl*. While not apparently having a direct or definable influence on Hogarth, Lauron anticipated his particular vein of realism by nearly half a century.[3]

Fig 11 Marcellus Lauron
Figure of a servant
Pen and ink $3\frac{1}{2} \times 2\frac{1}{8}$ inches
Fitzwilliam Museum, Cambridge

Fig 10 Marcellus Lauron *An Execution at Tyburn* Pencil and brown wash $9\frac{1}{4} \times 10\frac{3}{4}$ inches
Pepysian Library, Magdalene College, Cambridge

The immediate stimulus for the publication of a series of engraved London cries may have been J. Bonnart's *Cris de Paris* which preceded Lauron's *Cryes* by a year or two and with which there are some similarities, or even the engravings after Annibale Carracci's drawings for *Arti di Bologna* of 1646 or 1661, to which there is only, however, an occasional and probably fortuitous resemblance. The fact that the captions for the Lauron plates are in French and Italian as well as English indicates an attempt by the publisher, Pierce Tempest, to increase his sales by appealing to markets already familiar with the genre.

The actual origin of some of the plates however is far from simple. None has any apparent relation, except in subject, to earlier English woodcut series,[1] and it seems reasonable to suppose that the plates of street criers are, with sidelong glances at Bonnart, realistic representations of the figures to be seen in the London streets. Fourteen plates, which are, I think, the ones added in the edition of the autumn of 1688 and in 1689 (see Appendix III, pp 96–7) depict *Spanish Don, Squire of Alsatia, Mountabanck*, a courtezan, rope dancers and others, all with clearcut theatrical associations. James Granger, in 1806,[2] identified a number of the characters, including

[1] In 'Illustrations of Social Life III: Street Cries', *Shakespeare Survey*, Cambridge, 1960, vol. 13, pp106–10, where F. P. Wilson lists all the series before 1660 known to him.

[2] James Granger (continued to 1727 by Mark Noble), *Biographical History* – – – (1806), pp583–4.

Fig 12 Marcellus Lauron *Sword and Dagger Guard* (drawing for Plate 8 of *The Art of Defence*)
Pencil and brown wash 7 × 11⅝ inches British Museum

1 S. J. Gudlaugsson in *De Komedianten bij Jan Steen – – –* , The Hague, 1945, figs. 16 and 17, compares this painting with an engraving of *The Infallible Mountebank* (British Museum *Catalogue of Personal and Political Satires*, vol. I, no. 1032), in which the figure of the mountebank is copied from Lauron.

2 There are eight drawings with theatrical associations attributed to Lauron in the British Museum, seven of Commedia dell' Arte characters and one of a puppet showman. They are catalogued by E. Croft-Murray and P. Hulton, *Catalogue of British Drawings*, vol. 1, pp405–7, under 'Marcellus II Laroon' (Lauron) but with some doubt about the attribution. They came from the Strawberry Hill sale, 23rd June, 1842, lot 1251, (cont. p.17)

Mountebank, whom he describes as 'Hans Buling, a Dutchman who was well known in London as a mountebank . . . extremely fantastical in his dress . . . attended by a monkey which he had trained up to act the part of Jack Pudding . . .'. But the *Mountebank* is closely enough related to the figure of a quack doctor in a painting attributed to Eglon van der Neer[1] as to cast doubt on Granger's identification. The Dutch painting appears to be earlier than the late sixteen-eighties and Lauron could have taken his figure direct from the painting or from a copy or version of it. How much this invalidates a suggestion that some of the other theatrical and street characters represent true denizens of the London half-world it is difficult to say as I cannot point to such prototypes for any of the other plates.[2]

Lauron's *Cryes* appear to have had no influence on later English Cries, neither Paul Sandby's many drawings and set of etchings of 1760 nor Francis Wheatley's paintings and engravings of some thirty years later having more than an occasional fortuitous resemblance. The difference between the sets of Lauron and Wheatley has been well defined by John Steegman in *The Rule of Taste from George I to George IV* when he compares the latter's 'ever-popular *Cries of London*, wherein fishwives and flower-

Fig 13 Marcellus Lauron *A Gallant and his Lady* Mezzotint 6⅛ × 5¾ inches

'Pantomimical Characters dancing, singing etc. very spirited by an anonymous artist', twenty-four in all, but only these eight are now known. Although some are indented for transfer no engravings directly from the drawings have been traced. The Mezzetino was used, however, with minor alterations - *Coeuré del Prud'hon Sculpt* – in *La Galerie Théâtrale* in 1873. They have certain resemblances to the engravings of the Cryes but are not very close in style to the drawings known to be by Lauron and I think they are not by him.

Since this note was written Mr Croft-Murray has informed me of the discovery of a number of engravings corresponding with these drawings published by J. Mariette one of which, the Pulcinella, is inscribed *Bérain inv.* and lettered 'Deschars, danseur de l'Académie royale de musique, en habit de Polichinel, au divertissement de Villeneuve-Saint-Georges (1er septembre 1692)'. It seems therefore certain that the drawings should now be given to Jean Berain I (1640–1711).

sellers move through the streets with the sweet grace of Lady Hamilton in her Romney days, and the series of the same subject by Marcellus Laroon three generations earlier which are strong, individual, characteristic and convincingly true, though far from sweet'.

Numerous engravings, etchings and mezzotints by or after Lauron were published during these years; the subjects widely various – innocuous scenes of conversation and music-making, and street brawls, others frankly bawdy or lascivious, *A Gallant and his Lady* [Fig 13], *The Proposal*, *The Brothel* and one of a naked woman looking at herself by candlelight, and an occasional 'history'. A painting of *A Lady at Confession* was sold in Mr Graham's sale in 1771,[1] of which subject there are at least three different mezzotints. Pierce Tempest, the publisher, refers to one of these in a letter to Francis Place on 9th January, 1685/6:

'Yors I recd though the ladys have solely left painting *Mezzotintos* yet they doe sell a little especially fancy's Heads & bawdy soe I am provideing 3 or four new ones Against the Terme 2 Queens a new Confession 2 Fancys after *Laroone*, a Gent has Lent me a *Presbyterian Meeting* of the same Mar, wch *Van Somer* is Etching & Graveing together it will be rather bigger than the *Quakers* . . .'[2]

1 *Hist. MSS. Comm. Ailesbury*, 15R. App. pt.7, pp204–6.
2 British Museum, Stowe MS. 746. f.98. printed in H. M. Hake, 'Some contemporary records relating to Francis Place – – –', *Walpole Society*, vol. X, p65. Copies of a print of *The Presbyterian Conventicle* are in the Print Room of the British Museum and in the Pepysian Library. This print, mainly etched with a few engraved lines, is bigger than Heemskerck's Quaker meetings, and some of the figures recall Lauron's style. J. E. Wessely (*Catalogue of engravings by Paul van Somer*, R. Naumann's *Archiv für die zeichnenden Künste* – – –, vol. XVI, 1870, p64, no. 100) records a print with the names of Lauron, van Somer and Tempest. It seems likely that the two known examples are a re-issue with the names replaced by inscriptions.

Other similar subjects are of a monk scourging a young woman and the converse *The Bully Flogg'd*. Tempest's reference to the *Presbyterian Meeting* is of some interest as it provides a link with Egbert van Heemskerck, the chief exponent of pictures of Quaker meetings, whose style in fancies and bawdies is fairly close to Lauron's. But Buckeridge's succinct comment on Heemskerck, that he 'after all fell far short of Brawer, Teniers and the rest of his noble fore-runners, in the study of sots-paradice' applies equally well to Lauron.

Lauron's competence in his varied activities implies a hard apprenticeship in early life. He is said by Buckeridge to have been taught by his father, then for a short time by a history painter at the Hague, and after coming to England by 'one La Zoon', of whom he thought little, and by Balthazar Fleshiers. It has been suggested that 'La Zoon' was perhaps Lely's assistant Sonnius or Zonias; or a slip of the pen may have turned La Roon (one of the variant spellings) into La Zoon, so perhaps Buckeridge's equivocation 'One La Zoon' is the happiest solution after all. Balthazar Fleshiers, one of a family of painters, and probably the son of another Balthazar of Antwerp, was primarily a painter of sea-pieces and portraits. He seems to have had no impact on Lauron, and Vertue may be nearer the mark when he says that Lauron 'made improvements by the strength of his own genius mostly'. This view is echoed by Buckeridge who was sufficiently impressed to write:

'When he came to work for himself, he made it his endeavour to follow nature very close, so that his manner was wholly his own. He was a general painter, and imitated other Masters hands exactly well. He painted well, both in great and little, and was an exact draftsman; but he was chiefly famous for drapery, wherein he exceeded most of his contemporaries. He was likewise fam'd for pictures in little, commonly call'd conversation pieces'.[1]

1 B. Buckeridge, *Essay*, p396.

THE CRYES
of the City of
LONDON
Drawne after the Life.

Les Cris
de la Ville de
Londres
Desfignez apres la Nature.

L'Arti Comuni
che vanno p.
Londra
Fatte dal Naturale.

P. Tempest excudit

Cum Privilegie

First Title from *The Cryes of The City of London*

2 *A Sow Gelder*

3 *Any Card matches or Savealls*

4 *Pretty Maids Pretty Pinns Pretty Women*

5 *Ripe Strawberryes*

6 *A Bed Matt or a Door Matt*

7 *Buy a fine Table Basket*

8 *Ha Ha Ha Poor Jack*

9 *Buy my Dish of great Eeles*

10 *Buy a fine singing Bird*

11 *Buy any Wax or Wafers*

12 *Fine Writeing Inke*

13 *A Merry new Song*

14 *Old Shooes for Some Broomes*

15 *Hott Bak'd Wardens Hott*

16 *Small Coale*

17 *Maids any Cunny Skinns*

18 *Buy a Rabbet a Rabbet*

19 *Buy a Fork or a Fire Shovel*

20 *Chimney Sweep*

21 *Crab Crab any Crab*

22 *Oh Rare Shoe*

23 *The merry Milk Maid*

24 *The merry Fidler*

25 *Lilly white Vinegar 3 pence a quart*

26 *Buy my Dutch Biskets*

27 *Ripe Speragas*

28 *Maids buy a Mapp*

29 *Buy my fat Chickens*

30 *Buy my Flounders*

31 *Old Cloaks Suits or Coats*

32 *Fair Lemons & Oranges*

33 *Old Chaires to mend*

34 *Twelve Pence a Peck Oysters*

35 *Troope every one one*

36 *Old Satten Old Taffety or Velvet*

THE CRYES
of the City of
LONDON
Drawne after the Life.

Les Cris
de la Ville de
Londres
Dessignez apres la Nature.

L'Arti Comuni
che vanno p̄
Londra
Fatte dal Naturale.

P. Tempest excudit.

Cum Privilegio

37 Second title page

38 *Buy a new Almanack*

39 *Buy my fine singing Glasses*

40 *Any Kitchin Stuffe have you maids*

41 *Knives Combs or Inkhornes*

42 *Four for Six pence Mackrell*

43 *Any work for John Cooper*

44 *4 Paire for a Shilling Holland Socks*

45 *Colly Molly Puffe*

46 *Six pence a pound fair Cherryes*

47 *Knives or Cisers to Grinde*

48 *Long Threed Laces Long & Strong*

49 *Remember the Poor Prisoners*

50 *The Squire of Alsatia*

51 *London Curtezan*

52 *Madam Creswell*

53 *Merry Andrew*

33

54　*A Brass Pott or an Iron Pott to mend*

55　*Buy my 4 Ropes of Hard Onyons*

56　*Londons Gazette here*

57　*Buy a White Line, a Jack Line, or a Cloathes Line*

58 *Any Old Iron take money for*

59 *Delicate cowcumbers to pickle*

60 *Any Bakeing Peares*

61 *New River Water*

62 *The Spanish Don*

63 *Merry Andrew on the Stage*

64 *The famous Dutch Woman*

65 *Mountabanck*

66 *The famous Dutch Woman*

67 *Josephus Clericus*

68 *Clark the English Posture Master*

69 *The London Begger*

70 *John the Quaker*

71 *The London Quaker*

72 *Oliver C: Porter*

73 *A Nonconformist Minister*

74 *Frater Mendicans*

Fig 14

1 LIFE

The Muses had given Laroon the pencil of an artist but the pen of a clerk, and his factual autobiography, which covers nearly ten years with the words 'we still went on with our painting' and includes the remark that 'I leave out all private occurrences', is the despair of the later biographer. 'I write' he tells us nevertheless 'the following memorandums, not as a regular account of battles, sieges, or other actions I have seen, but for the satisfaction of my particular friends, who, perhaps, might be desirous to know how I have spent my life'.

In the early summer of 1697, his father being willing that he 'should see foreign parts', he was made one of six pages to Sir Joseph Williamson about to go as a plenipotentiary to the Congress of Ryswick. Williamson and his suite sailed in June but the crossing was delayed by a violent and dangerous storm and off-shore wind, and it was not until some days later that they landed at Hellevoetsluis for the Hague, where they stayed for the three months which elapsed before the signing of the treaty. Laroon hardly refers to painting in his autobiography, failing to mention paintings or painters at the Hague or during his subsequent stay in Venice. It seems unlikely that he would have spent several months in each of these still important artistic centres without meeting painters and seeing paintings; and one can perhaps assume some familiarity with what was to be seen in both places.

Meanwhile at home his father had arranged to place him as page to the Earl of Manchester, Envoy to the Venetians, who was to pass through the Hague on his way to Venice. Lauron's ability to get what he wanted for his son suggests that he had some influence in diplomatic and aristocratic circles. The intermediary in this appointment was perhaps Kneller, who had painted the Countess of Manchester some years earlier. The long journey across Europe, with the privileges and comforts of diplomacy, would be an exciting adventure for an eighteen-year-old; something of a poor man's grand tour. In his own words:

'We were one and twenty in family, almost all English. Mr. Stanyan was then with us as Secretary to the Embassy. We passed through Cleve to Cologne, where we all embarked on board two large vessels (fastened together, with all our baggage) on the Rhine, and were drawn against that strong stream by a great number of horses to Frankfurt, from whence my Lord and all his suite travelled in different voitures by Innsbruck, and through the Tyrol mountains to Merano; from whence we were transported in proper vessels to Venice'.

The Earl's letters reiterate the maddening slowness with which things were done in Venice: 'I find they propose to do all the honour that is possible or ever hath been done

Fig 14 opposite
Marcellus Laroon *Self-Portrait*
Oil on canvas 32 × 26 inches
Mr & Mrs Paul Mellon

to a king but the way they transact business is slow': so slow in fact that not until a month later did the Earl with his entire suite, make his ceremonial entry in, according to Laroon, 'very magnificent gondolas, two whereof were very richly carved, gilt and ornamented'. In a vivid description of the Public Entry of an ambassador, a contemporary writer evokes the formality and hedonism of Venice at the turn of the century. The whole of the ambassador's suite, 'his Domesticks, the Consul, all the merchants and others of his Nation . . . to the lowest of his Servants that are out of Livery', took part in the ceremony, going early in the morning to a convent on the island of Santo Spirito. There they were visited by a body of Senators with whom, in their gondolas, they returned for the reception by the Doge, an affair of high formality with many speeches and the presentation of credential letters. For two days the town was 'in mask, and there is Musick all night in the Ambassador's House, where all who will come, are entertain'd, with Wine, Coffee, and all sorts of Refreshments, so that crouds of Masks go and come continually; small Guns or Mortars are fired about the House, etc. There are Trumpets and Drums; and great quantities of Loaves of Bread, and Pitchers with Wine are given away to the common People, who croud about the Palace'.[1] In spite of this impressive reception and the elaborate entertainment by the Doge and seignory for nearly four months, the Earl's mission was unsuccessful, and he returned with his task unaccomplished; but for these four months the members of his suite, from their palace on the Cannaregio, were not only familiar with Venice, in its already declining splendour, but enjoyed, according to Laroon, the opportunity of seeing 'their operas and all that was usually shown to strangers'. To amplify Laroon's bald statement we must go to two travellers, Maximilian Misson[2] and Limojon de Saint Didier,[3] whose accounts of Venice, although written some twenty years earlier, may be taken as reflecting conditions at the time of Laroon's visit to this slowly changing city. Misson, illustrating the special opportunities in Venice for the study of painting, after comments on particular pictures, Veronese's *Marriage at Cana* in the Refectory of San Giorgio Maggiore, Titian's *Presentation of the Virgin* in the Scuola della Caritá and his *St Peter Martyr* in SS. Giovanni e Paolo, continues: 'Venice is perhaps the only City in Europe where young Painters may best study the Beauties of Nature. There are two Academies where there are always naked Persons of both sexes to be viewed and which are often on the Stage together and in what posture they please to put them. Everybody may come in there'. There were, in fact, many more than two so-called *accademie* which were really private studios where artists could work from the model.

As music was to be a lifelong enthusiasm for Laroon it is not surprising that he should have taken the opportunity to see Venetian opera. As with painting, no other city in Europe could offer such chances. There were then seven opera companies giving seasons of from twelve to thirty weeks. Between 1637, when the first opera house was opened, and 1700, nearly 400 operas were performed. Opinion about the quality of these performances varies. Limojon, in 1674, praises the theatres, the décor and costumes, the voices and the orchestra; but Misson fifteen years later says that the costumes were poor, that there were no dances nor any illumination except for a few candles, but agrees with Limojon about the voices and 'some excellent Ayres'. Laroon's arrival in Venice was just before the opening of the Carnival which was held from Epiphany until Shrove Tuesday; so the masquerades and performances of the Commedia dell' Arte would be alternatives to the academies and the opera houses. The Commedia performances, according to Misson, were 'ridiculous and wretched

1 C. Cole, *Memoirs of Affairs of State* – 1697–1708, 1733, p13. The painting by Luca Carlevaris of Manchester's magnificent entry on his second visit in 1707 is now in the City of Birmingham Art Gallery. Reproduced in W. Nisser, 'Lord Manchester's Reception at Venice', *Burlington Magazine*, vol. 70, 1937, pp30–34.

2 M. Misson, *A New Voyage to Italy*, English translation 1695, passim.
3 Limojon de St Didier, *La Ville et la République de Venise*, 1680, passim.

Buffooneries (where) the most lascivious Bawdy thing is pronounced in the most expressive terms', but Misson's condemnation was a minority opinion.

On the slow return journey, after passing through Padua, Vicenza, Verona, Brescia, Bergamo, Milan and Vercelli, the Earl's suite stayed for three days at Turin and were then delayed by heavy snow while crossing the Mont Cenis pass. They then travelled to Montmélian, on the Rhône to Lyons, and reaching Paris, early in May, stayed there only a few days before continuing their journey to London. Laroon's narrative continues:

'As my father's circumstances were not such as would enable him to give us fortunes, we were obliged to learn to earn a living; we then went on in painting; but a quarrel I had with my younger brother, (for we were three), which I thought unjustly supported on his side by my father, made me resolve to leave him. Having some knowledge in music, I threw myself on the theatre in Drury-Lane, about the year 1698, where I continued, not as an actor, but a singer, for about two years.'

Well-trained in music, equipped with a 'noble strong voice', and familiar with Venetian opera, burlesque and masquerade, he would be a useful addition to the company at Drury Lane which Colley Cibber, a member of it, contrasts with its rival at Lincoln's Inn Fields: '*Betterton's* People (however good in their Kind) were most of them too far advanc'd in Years to mend; and tho' we, in *Drury Lane*, were too young to be excellent, we were not too old to be better'.[1]

Only one performance by a singer named Laroon is recorded within two years of 1698, when, with Mrs Lindsey, he sang 'Plenty mirth and gay delight' in the operatic entertainment *The Grove* at Drury Lane about February 1699/1700.[2] There are however between 1702 and 1706, six performances recorded in which 'Mr Laroon' took part. It appears that this singer was one of those engaged for the more general part of the programme but with occasional roles in opera. Typical of these mixed entertainments are:

' "The Bath, or the Western Lass" At the Desire of several Persons of Quality and for the benefit of the Author . . . reviv'd . . . intermix'd with Vocal Musick and Dancing, particularly a Song beginning Let the dreadful Engines etc, performed by Mr. Leveridge, a comical Dialogue by him and Mrs. Lindsey, beginning with Since the Times are so bad etc. Another perform'd by Mr. Laroone and Mr. Hughes, beginning Sing, Sing, all ye Muses'.

' . . . a Consort of Musick by the best Masters wherein the Famous Signiora Joanna Maria will sing several Songs . . . With several New Entertainments of Dancing . . . To which will be added a Comedy of two Acts only . . . And several Entertainments of Singing by Mr. Leveridge, Mr. Laroon and Mr. Hughes'.[3]

It is just a little uncertain whether this 'Mr Laroon' was Marcellus or his brother John, who was painter and musician but not as far as we know a singer, and who was also employed at Drury Lane but in the orchestra. The initial of the singer is given once as 'J', once as 'F' but never as 'M'. Although Laroon was not always reliable with dates it is difficult to ignore his statement that he remained on the stage for about two years after 1698, but it is significant that none of the above performances took place during his first spell of army service in 1704, or after his regular service began in 1707. On the balance I think it likely that the singer was Marcellus.

John Laroon seems to have been something of a ne'er-do-well if Jacob Campo Weyerman, who was in England in about 1718 to 1720, is to be relied on. He was an accomplished portrait painter, Weyerman says, trained by Michael Dahl, who could have earned 'four or five guineas a day' but for his fatal attraction to music, 'scraping

1 Colley Cibber, *An Apology for the Life of Mr Colley Cibber*, 1740, p245.

2 In a personal communication from Professor Emmett L. Avery.

3 These two performances were at Drury Lane, on 8th December, 1702, and 23rd January, 1703. Laroon's other appearances were: at Drury Lane, 1st February, 1703, in one act of the *Faerie Queen*; at Drury Lane, on 12th February, 1703, 'singing by Mr Laroon and Mr Hughs particularly a Two-part song compos'd by the late Mr Henry Purcell'; at York Buildings on 29th March 1704; at the Queen's Theatre on 7th March, 1706, when the role of Sylvander in *The Temple of Love* was sung by Laroon with the initial given variously as 'F' or 'J'; at the Queen's Theatre in July 1706 and perhaps earlier in the same year in *The Kingdom of Birds*. Information about these appearances comes mainly from E. L. Avery, *The London Stage*, pt.2, vol. I, and also from C. Burney, *A General History of Music*, (1776–1789), 1935 edition, vol. II, p985; G. Grove, *Dictionary of Music and Musicians*, 1880 edition, vol. II, p92; J. Downes, *Roscius Anglicanus*, (1708), 1886 edition, p49.

on the four-stringed bass'. He was employed by the Duke of Beaufort at Badminton and there is said to have painted both the Duke and Duchess, but his 'Spanish [sic] idleness, British drunkenness and Flemish carelessness' eventually led to his being thrown out of the Duke's employment, and to his return to play the bass at Drury Lane. He laughed at Weyerman's admonitions replying:

'Campo, you are talking about what is beyond your comprehension; there is no delight in love or in art to compare with music. Music masters the soul and the soul rules all the passions. But just as beauty is no beauty without virtue and music is no music unless accompanied by art, so will I who am a superlative musician, practise the art as long as there is breath in my body.'[1]

Weyerman's account is confirmed in one particular by Vertue who says that John was a pupil of Dahl's.[2]

John was sole executor after his father's death 'of a consumption' at Richmond early in 1702. Lauron left his property to be shared between his children and Mrs Burgess; Marcellus receiving his amethyst ring, gilded snuff box set with rubies, and one silver spoon, and John his sealing ring, silver watch, silver tobacco box, one silver spoon and his bass viol. His three sons received all his limnings, drawings, pictures and paintings, to be divided equally between them, some or all of which were sold many years later in 1725.[3] Provision was also made for his daughter Elizabeth who was then only thirteen, two-thirds of the residue of his estate being left to her and her brother James and one-third to John and Marcellus.

After leaving the stage, of which he had grown tired, Marcellus practised painting, he tells us, until 1707, when he 'resolved to carry arms'. Weyerman publishes however, after translating it into Dutch, a letter signed *N. Laroon* to the writer's brother Jan, which purports to have been written on the eve of the battle of Schellenberg in 1704, where the writer was serving as a volunteer. Weyerman's accompanying description of 'N' Laroon's career leaves no doubt that he is referring to Marcellus. It seems at first sight unlikely that Laroon would have omitted his earliest experience of the Army from his reminiscences, which describe, in fair detail, the various campaigns in which he served; but he failed to mention the battle of Malplaquet, at which he was present, and some later service in Ireland; and a number of dates which he gives are open to correction. It is an interesting letter, not so much for its content, as for its lively, humorous and slightly irreverent idiom: and as the only letter of his which has survived, it has, even in double translation, its own peculiar value.[4]

Dear Brother,
          Now I am actively engaged with the preparation of my ammunition pouch and other instruments of war so as to be shot through the head on the morrow at the storming of the French and Bavarian lines. I expect to get a standard there or bite the dust, for in my present occupation of a volunteer killer, I value an honourable death higher than a dishonourable life. Death is not so terrible as people would have it, for death is the end of all fears and the beginning of bliss, and no man dies so willingly as he who walks honourably along this hateful road of transitory life. Death, brother Jan, is the shears that cuts the thread of man's cares, but dishonour is the beginning of all cares. But brother Jan, because I know you are not such a theologian as the bishop of Cangor,[5] I shall tell you that Death is divided into three parts like our regimental drill. The first Death is the parting between the soul and the body, as well as the decomposition of the body until the day of Judgement. The second is the Death of sin, because that man is hailed as dead who is laid to rest in sin. And the last is eternal Death, to which the godless shall be condemned until the end of time.
          So much of religion have I gathered in the company of the general's chaplain, and if I can gather a company by it before the end of the expedition, I shall be in every way pleased with my first campaign.

1 J. C. Weyerman, *De Leevens-Beschryvingen der Nederlandsche Konst-Schilders*, 1729–69, vol. IV, 2nd pagination 28–33.

2 Vertue also says that he drew a portrait of Charles Christian Reisen.

3 According to Horace Walpole this sale was on 24th February, 1725, when 'the son [Laroon] sold his collection of pictures (among which were many painted by his father)'. No copy of the catalogue is known to exist.

4 See Appendix IV for the letter as printed by Weyerman.

5 'Cangor' is certainly a misreading of Bangor. The preferment of John Evans to the Bishopric of Bangor in 1702 seems to have caused both dismay and amusement (see *Dictionary of National Biography*).

Farewell, brother Jan, I am getting sleepy, and so I will avail myself of the sleep now, because at break of day, the artillery, the kettle-drum, the cymbals, the drums, the trumpets and the funeral music of the heavy and light musketry shall keep all sleep out of your brother's eyes.

The volunteer   N. Laroon

Schellenberg,
the night before the battle,
in July 1704.

Laroon's autobiography describes clearly, if undramatically, the more important events during the twenty-five years that he was, with intervals, in the Army, beginning with his attachment to a battalion of the First Regiment of Foot Guards, then serving in Flanders under Colonel Charles Gorsuch. Proceeding to Holland he writes:

'I was so happy as to have for my friend Colonel Molesworth, aide-de-camp to the Duke of Marlborough: with him I had the favour to pass the sea in the yacht with the Duke, to whom I was introduced on board. We arrived safe in Holland.

I then joined the battalion of Guards, with Colonel Gorsuch, and did sometimes duty in the regiment as a cadet; and we took the field. That campaign we had neither battle nor seige: the enemy, as it was rumoured, had formed a design to attack the Duke of Marlborough's quarters, to carry him off in the night. His quarters being some distance from the grand army, and covered only by the battalion of Guards, the out-guards and sentries were doubled, and a sentry was to be placed at the door of the Duke's bedchamber. I desired to have that post, and chose not to be relieved the whole night, which passed without any disturbance from the enemy'.

After this campaign, on 20th September 1707, the Duke gave him a commission as Lieutenant to Captain Archibald Hamilton, in the Earl of Orkney's first battalion. Laroon was to serve in this famous regiment, the Royal Scots, until 1709. As a result of the heavy losses at Almanza, a recruiting campaign was initiated and a Lieutenant and an Ensign from each regiment, Laroon representing the Royal Scots, were sent to England to attempt to raise the necessary complement of recruits. Returning to Flanders in the following Spring with ten recruits he rejoined his regiment in time for the campaign leading up to the battle of Oudenarde in July 1708. The Royal Scots formed part of a division of twenty battalions commanded by the Duke of Argyll. The musketry fire was said to be exceedingly fierce, and violent hand to hand fighting took place along the whole front. The regiment was ordered to dislodge the enemy, who had posted themselves in strong enclosures, and this they did with very small loss.

After Oudenarde the Royal Scots were part of the covering force for the siege of Lille, and among other duties were engaged in gathering contributions from Arras and the surrounding district. Laroon was in the battalion which was detailed from the covering army to protect an important convoy bringing vital supplies from Ostend, without which the successful siege of Lille would be impossible. This small force, commanded by Major General Webb, took advantage of the wooded hillsides of the Wynendael valley through which the French attacking force had to pass. The French were routed, losing 3000 men to the Allied loss of 1000, and the convoy reached the besieging army without damage. Laroon was slightly wounded, being struck on the forehead and left arm by spent musket balls, the resulting contusions, he tells us, taking a month to heal. The citadel of Lille surrendered in December, thus ending a campaign where, according to Corporal Deane, whose natural gift for vivid exposition, in contrast to Laroon's prosaic style, did not always make for clarity, 'we were continually fateagued and bugbeard out of our lives by those who had as much will to fight as to be hanged'.[1]

1 J. M. Deane, *Journal of the Campaign in Flanders, 1708*, 1846, p20.

Fig 15 Marcellus Laroon *Execution of Deserters – at Meldert Camp 1707*
Black and brown inks on pencil 7½ × 10⅞ inches John Richardson

To close this campaign, Ghent was besieged, and here Laroon was again wounded, this time more seriously:

'At the siege of Ghent I had the advanced-guard at the opening of the trenches. The morning after the trench was completed, I was in conversation with some of our officers and some of the battalion of Guards: it being a very thick fog, one of the town came and fired among us, and shot me through the shoulder, and the next day I was sent to Brussels'.

The Royal Scots spent the early months of 1709 in winter quarters, where Laroon joined them after convalescing from his wounds. After an uneventful spring and early summer both battalions joined in what was to be one of the most fearful sieges of the whole war. Towards the end of June Tournai was invested and a month later the town yielded and 4,000 men under the command of Surville withdrew into the citadel, which according to Richard Kane was 'one of the best fortify'd Places by Art that is in the World'.[1] Laroon again commanded the advance guard at the opening of the trenches and served in them during the whole siege, on battering pieces and bomb batteries. The underground defences were more formidable than those visible and the Allied forces in the trenches were in their turn undermined by the French working from the Citadel. Constant explosions buried many men and in one no fewer than four hundred were said to have perished. Laroon was unscathed when the Citadel capitulated. Immediately afterwards the army marched towards Mons and met the French forces at Malplaquet. Laroon does not himself mention the battle of Malplaquet but his name appears in the Army lists of serving officers – so it can only be assumed that he had one of his lapses of memory at this point in his reminiscences.[2]

1 R. Kane, *Campaigns of King William and Queen Anne*, 1745, p83.

2 C. Dalton, *English Army Lists and Commission Registers, 1661–1714*, 1892–1904, vol. VI, p322.

Towards the end of 1709 he was back in London but only for a short time. James Craggs the younger, whom Laroon may have met when Craggs, Resident at the court at Barcelona, was carrying military information between Marlborough and General Stanhope, invited him to join Stanhope's forces in Spain; accordingly Laroon gave up his commission in the Royal Scots, left London and accompanied by Craggs's secretary went post from Utrecht through Germany to Genoa, where fifteen days later, they embarked on a man-of-war with Stanhope and Craggs and sailed to Barcelona, arriving there in May 1710. Early in the summer, having no commission, Laroon was appointed by Stanhope as Deputy Quartermaster-General of the English troops, in which employment he served the whole campaign. It is unlike him to under-estimate his achievements and perhaps transcription of his manuscript by the unreliable Smith is responsible for the discrepancy between his statement and the official list of officers taken prisoner at Brihuega which includes 'Qr-Mr-Gen Mr Laroon', there being no mention of a deputy for the post.[1] Curious as it seems, he appears therefore to have held, for some time at least, this important position which, five years earlier, under Peterborough, had been held by George Carpenter, now Lieutenant-General and second-in-command to Stanhope.

1 *Ibid.* p386.

Soon after Laroon's arrival, Stanhope, with his command of 4,000 men, joined Starhemberg, the Allied commander, at Balaquer, which was shortly after attacked by the Spanish. Laroon's account of the battle differs from the usual one because, I think, of his confusion of Balaquer with the following encounter at Almenara, when he describes a cavalry charge, led by Stanhope, which according to other reliable accounts, took place at the former. Of Balaquer Laroon writes:

'The enemy, whose army was superior to ours, marched to Balaquer, where we were encamped. Maréchal Starhemberg drew up our troops upon some hills, and posted the army advantageously. At the foot of the eminence was an old, demolished fort, where he had placed a good detachment, and a battery of cannon. The enemy came on in two lines upon an open plain, and the battery from an old fort played upon them with success. The hills were not so difficult of ascent as to hinder the horse of both armies from gaining the top, where their cavalry and ours faced each other for two hours: Colonel Borgard had planted a battery, from which he fired with great slaughter among the Spanish horse, who stood it with incredible resolution for a considerable time. The enemy finding us in good posture to receive them, declined the attack, and marched away'.

Stanhope then, with the advance detachment of cavalry and grenadiers, reached Alfaraz first in a race with the Spanish, enabling Starhemberg and the whole army to cross the river Noguera. Laroon, describing the battle of Almenara, continues:

'Upon our march we saw the enemy advancing very fast to get possession of a high hill. We marched with all expedition also, and were met on the height of the mountain, upon a plain scarce wide enough to draw up our foot in two lines. The horse on both sides advanced in two lines; General Stanhope, turning to our men, cried out 'In the name of God we will beat them!' and charged the enemy with great resolution, broke through, and routed them entirely; many were driven, horse and man, down the precipice; and had not night come on, their army would have suffered greatly: unhappily, one of our batteries playing mistook Count Nassau's regiment for the enemy, and by a shot, Count Nassau, a cornet, and a dragoon were killed.

At the battle of Saragossa, as I had no commission, I desired to go on a volunteer with Colonel du Bourgay's regiment of foot, then commanded by Lieutenant-Colonel Burgess, to whom I applied. He made me a compliment, and lent me his own fusee, bayonet and cartouch-box. We lay on our arms all night. I was placed on the right of the grenadiers; our regiment was in the front line. Upon the discharge of a piece of artillery, which was the sign for advancing towards the enemy, we marched forward to meet them, they, at the same time, advancing to meet us. We marched upon a rising ground, and did not see the enemy till we were within twenty yards of him. We had orders to receive their fire and accordingly went on with our arms recovered; but being so near, it obliged one side to begin, which they did, and gave us their full discharge, but did not kill many of our men, for most of their shot went over our heads, and killed more in Dormer's regiment, which was in our rear. We then levelled at them, and sent a well-directed discharge among them, which broke their ranks, and they fled. We pursued them with great slaughter a great way, and took about five or six thousand prisoners. We were then masters of Saragossa'.

The march to Madrid, which had been evacuated by Philip who took with him the government officials, grandees, and, it is said, 30,000 of the population, presented no difficulties and there was no opposition. The city was entered towards the end of September, and then Stanhope's troubles began. Worse than unco-operative the inhabitants were actively dangerous and supplies from the surrounding country unobtainable. When the retreat from Madrid started Stanhope wrote home to say that they had no supplies and no money to buy food, with 'the country about us all up in arms'. The allied armies were divided into three columns to aid foraging. Stanhope with the most easterly column, 'all which regiments were very weak by battles, sickness, and desertion', reached Brihuega, where he halted for the night. Vendôme, the French commander, had, unknown to Stanhope, caught up, and without warning the French and Spanish troops appeared on the surrounding hills. Describing the battle which, according to some authorities, was the fiercest of the whole campaign, Laroon writes:

'While we were at Brihuega, not having intelligence, being in an enemy's country, we were surprised and encompassed by the French and Spanish forces; General Stanhope immediately sent Captain Cosby (one of his aides-de-camp) to Maréchal Starhemberg, with an account of our situation. The enemy began to fire from several batteries of cannon, and with ease beat down an old Moorish wall of no strength. Our men were all dismounted, and defended bravely at the breach. The Scotch Guards suffered much; but notwithstanding the whole power of the enemy, if our men had not been scanty of ammunition, they had not entered the place. As we suspected no army near us, that article had been neglected.

During the preparations for our defence, General Stanhope, General Carpenter, Colonel Dormer, etc. etc., from a tower, were viewing their approaches: General Stanhope had ordered a parapet to be made for our men to fire over; he saw that it was not high enough, and sent me with his orders to have it raised higher. I had no way to go down to the officers but through the gateway, and down the side of a hill, quite exposed to the enemy; which I did, but received no hurt, though a good number of shot were levelled at me. I delivered the orders, and returned the same way, through the same fire, to the General, with the answer of the officer, that his orders should be obeyed; but it not being immediately done, I was a second time sent, and, by great good fortune, escaped many more shot that was discharged at me.

The Marshal not coming to our relief, the enemy having entered some parts of the town, General Stanhope ordered the chamade; and capitulated, that the generals and all the officers should keep their own equipages, but the troops to surrender prisoners of war, and give up all their horses and arms'.

After a short time in captivity at Valladolid, Stanhope, accompanied by his secretary, Arend Furley, Lieutenant-Colonel James Moyser, Captain Henry Killigrew and Laroon, went to Saragossa to negotiate the exchange of prisoners. Nothing having been settled after a month, they were sent to Najera, about midway between Valladolid and Saragossa, where they remained 'prisoners, with liberty to go out where we pleased to divert ourselves, about twenty months'. A treaty of exchange was settled in May 1711, but Stanhope and his suite remained in captivity due, it has been suggested, to the reluctance of the Tory government to have such an active and powerful Whig as Stanhope back in England before they must.

As soon as they were released, Laroon says:

'we passed by Pampeluna, over the Pyrenean Mountains, and came to Pau in Berne, where . . . we stayed till the ratification of the exchange of the prisoners was completed . . . We went from thence to Bordeaux, where at that time the Maréchal de Montrevel was Governor. General Stanhope and his suite were invited to dine with him; his entertainment was very noble. From Bordeaux, we travelled to Paris; myself and Captain Killigrew went post to Paris, and from thence to Calais, and passed the sea to Dover, and returned to London'.

Laroon's life in the army was to be interrupted for three years when, in August 1712, his regiment was disbanded and he was placed on half-pay. In the autumn after his return, with the intention perhaps of assuming or resuming the career of a professional painter, he became a member of the Academy of Painting which had been established in the previous year in a house in Queen's Street, Lincoln's Inn Fields.[1] Sir Godfrey Kneller, its first Governor, was assisted in the management of the Academy by twelve Directors who included Jonathan Richardson, the portraitist, Thornhill, Pellegrini and Louis Laguerre, the history and decorative painters, an engraver, a pastellist and a sculptor. Here Laroon would find himself in the company not only of eminent artists but of connoisseurs and dilletanti such as James Seymour, the banker and father of the like-named painter, Hugh Howard, the painter and connoisseur whom Laroon may have known at the Congress of Ryswick when Howard was page in the suite of the Earl of Pembroke, and, elected at the same time as Laroon, Richard Steele who, to show his appreciation of the honour, wrote his sophistical essay on English portraiture.[2] Also among the members were his friends Christian Reisen, the seal engraver, and Owen MacSwiney, the then manager of the Haymarket Theatre who, early in 1713, fled bankrupt to Venice where he established a flourishing picture trade; and it was here no doubt that George Vertue first came to know him.

1 Walpole Society, *Vertue VI*, pp168–170.

2 *The Spectator*, no. 555, 4th December, 1712.

The importance of Kneller's Academy in the formation of the English school has, like the ability of Kneller himself, received less than justice. It should be assessed more from Vertue's comment that 'from this school (being by all accounts the most formidable) (as yet) many young genius have distinguished themselves & given great hopes of becoming Flourishing men in this Kingdom' than from Hogarth's retrospective statement: 'The first place of this sort was begun about sixty years ago, by some gentlemen painters of the first rank, who, in their forms, imitated the Academy of France, but conducted their business with less fuss and solemnity; yet the little there was of it soon became the object of ridicule'.

Kneller's period of governorship lasted in fact for five years and he was then succeeded by Thornhill. Hogarth shows further his misunderstanding or dislike of the Academy by comparing it with the French Academy of Painting and Sculpture, an official and highly organised authoritarian institution, whose views Sir Antony Blunt has succinctly summed up as 'reason, rules and the best masters'. It would be absurd, if not impossible, to omit consideration of the French Academy from a history of French art; neither absurd nor impossible, but insensitive to the artistic climate of the early eighteenth century, to omit mention in a history of English art of Sir Godfrey's private academy of modest size and modest intention. For Laroon the Academy provided instruction, the use of a model and the company of his fellow artists, all of which he must have needed after five years campaigning.

There is no indication in Vertue's notes on the Academy whether Laroon was a regular attender and whether he remained a member during the three years that he was in London. No work is known which can be assigned to these years, except possibly the *Musical Assembly* [Plate 3] but this is more likely to have been painted after, rather than before, 1715. For whatever reason, no other trace of his activities has been found until July 1715, when, restive as usual and with his 'martial vigour' undiminished, he was commissioned as Captain-Lieutenant in Colonel William Stanhope's Dragoons. This was one of twenty-five regiments raised to deal with the threatened Jacobite invasion and the expected rising in Scotland and the West. Sent to the North, Stanhope's Dragoons were at Lancaster when in November they were ordered to join forces with other regiments under General Carpenter and General Wills to meet the rebels who, in their march from Scotland, had penetrated as far as Lancashire. Laroon writes:

'Our regiment only was at Lancaster. When the rebels advanced towards us, we retired to Preston, and from thence to Wigan, where General Wills joined us with several regiments of dragoons, and Colonel Preston's regiment of foot. We then marched towards the enemy, and met him in the road between Preston and Wigan. They had a design of turning off towards Manchester, but finding us so near them, retired with some precipitation to Preston, (without defending Ribble Bridge,) and barricaded the avenues; all the dragoons were dismounted, and the horses were linked together and put into the adjacent fields with a sufficient number of men to take care of them. General Wills then invested the place, and sent to Liverpool for two or three pieces of cannon to force the barricades. In the interim, he ordered an attack to be made by Preston's regiment and a good body of dragoons, but with bad success; they being quite exposed, and the enemy firing from behind the barricades, and from windows, and other holes under cover. They were obliged to retire with great loss. General Carpenter, with four regiments of dragoons, then joined us, and the enemy surrendered'.

This victory and the less decisive one of the Duke of Argyll at Sheriffmuir on the same day broke the back of the rebellion, although there was still much for the Government forces to do. Stanhope's regiment was consequently ordered to Scotland to join Argyll and

'went to Glasgow, and afterwards joined Lord Cadogan and the army at Stirling, and marched in very hard weather, towards the enemy. The Chevalier de St George [the Pretender] was with him; he did not stay to give battle, but embarked and went off to Montrose.

Their army then dispersed, and ours were sent to different quarters; but some time after, some clans were again in arms, upon which a sufficient number of troops were sent into the Highlands, and about five hundred dragoons. We marched to Badenoch, to the Blair of Athol; from thence to Inverness, where we encamped. The clans being dispersed, we marched towards Edinburgh, and Colonel Stanhope's regiment was quartered at Inerask, and Musselburgh. From thence to Dumfries, where we remained some time; then marched to England, and were quartered at York and the neighbouring towns'.

In January 1718 Laroon was promoted Captain; but in November of the same year the regiment was disbanded and he was placed on half-pay, on which, according to his own account, he remained for about eight years: 'Lord Cadogan got me the King's sign-manual, for the first troop of dragoons that should become vacant in any of the regiments then in Great Britain. I was disappointed of two'. There is however some confusion here, for in January 1723/24, after only five years, he was given a captaincy in Brigadier Kerr's Dragoons. Moreover his name is said to have appeared in the Commission Registers at Dublin as being appointed Captain in Munden's Dragoons in Ireland in 1719.[1] No record exists of his activities during this hiatus in his army service, but a second visit to Venice, although not mentioned by Vertue, Smith or elsewhere, would make more sense of the strong Venetian influences on his work of the twenties and thirties which will be discussed later.

His commission in Kerr's Dragoons, the 7th Hussars or Queen's Own, was to prove

[1] These Commission Registers perished when the Dublin Record Office was destroyed in 1922.

his last and least eventful. The regiment was employed largely in routine duties in Hampshire, Devonshire, Durham and Yorkshire, being stationed for some months at York, where it was reviewed in 1725 by Lt. Gen. Carpenter and in 1726 by Lt. Gen. Sir Charles Wills. Returning to London in 1727, it stood by to resist the Dutch but no embarkation took place, and in the same year it was reviewed by the King on Hounslow Heath. It continued in the South, Laroon serving with the rank of Captain, until 1732, when retiring 'his Majesty was graciously pleased to give me the pay of Captain of a troop'. And here, at the age of fifty-three, ended his long and far from mediocre career as a soldier.

He appears to have been more fortunate than most retiring officers in being allowed the full pay of a Captain – a weekly income of about four pounds – instead of the more usual half-pay. In spite of this not inconsiderable pension any loss to a retired officer with presumably little capital can be serious. Vertue must however be speaking comparatively when he says that Laroon 'lost much' in the Charitable Corporation, a great fraud which was described by a contemporary as 'a most unheard of Villainy ever projected, even worse in proportion than the fatal South Sea scheme'. Laroon's loss was £180 in this fund, ostensibly established 'for the relief of the Industrious Poor, by assisting them with small pledges at legal interest', which, after the flight of cashier and banker to France, was found to be deficient to the tune of over £400,000. Subscriptions to a lottery, held in 1734, to raise funds to compensate the defrauded, were large enough to pay back nearly half the losses, Laroon's share amounting to £87. 10. 0.[1]

Vertue suggests that although he 'scorn'd the name of being a professer' Laroon might have made a living out of painting, since 'he lately has amusd himself more particularly to painting & drawing. conversations. in small with much variety & pleasant entertainment of musick. some portraits in large from the life. whereby he woud not be uneasy if he coud, (stoop to it) now to make some benefit of it. which seems a little aukard to begin with, after 50 four or five'.[2] No doubt he did, then and later, sell paintings, but there is no record of his prices apart from Vertue's statement in 1732 that 'he has lately painted a very large family peice valud at several hundred pounds':[3] an exceptionally high figure in the light of prices charged by other painters. Of those comparable perhaps in status with Laroon the young Allan Ramsay in 1738 was charging only eight guineas for a head,[4] and Joseph Highmore, a year earlier, forty guineas for a full length.[5] Even Hogarth some years later, about 1746, received only £200 for his *Garrick as Richard the Third*,[6] which he recorded as being 'more than any English artist has received before for a single portrait.' It is difficult to understand then why Laroon was able to command so high a fee – the more so because Vertue expresses no surprise.

Another small source of income may have been some desultory picture dealing, for, although his name has not been found among the buyers in any annotated sale catalogues, he bought at least one picture for Sir Robert Walpole in 1729. There were probably few painters who did not at some time in their lives take part in the vast picture trade which had resulted from the accepted necessity of connoisseurship as one of a gentleman's accomplishments. This trade was riddled with dishonesty; the most notable frauds usually engineered by professional or semi-professional dealers, who knew best how to take advantage of the remarkable opportunities offered them when furnishing the new homes of the nobility and gentry: as Gwyn remarks in 1749 in his *Essay in Design*, 'We often hear of a sum given for a single work of an ancient

1 The affairs of the Charitable Corporation are frequently reported and discussed in *The Gentleman's Magazine* from March 1731 until May 1734 when a list of losses and allowances was published.

2 Walpole Society, *Vertue III*, 65.

3 *Ibid.* p64.

4 A. Smart, *The Life and Art of Allan Ramsay*, 1952, p37.
5 York Public Library, *York Chamberlains' Accounts*, 1738, f.14r. for the portrait of Sir John Lister Kaye. The portrait is in the Mansion House, York.
6 R. B. Beckett, *Hogarth*, 1949, p16.

master that equals the revenue of a gentleman's estate and sometimes, in these cases, the ignorance of the purchaser, or the knavery of the seller, imposes a copy of little value instead of the original'.

Laroon does not appear to have done any major dealing, perhaps because his only known attempt seems to have been unsuccessful. The account is best set out as it is found in Vertue's notebook:[1]

'Capt Laron having recommended & bought for Sr. Rob.
Walpole. a painting of the Madona Child & St. Elizabeth.
which he judged to be painted by Vandyke. of which several
painters Judges, etc did not. think.so. (particularly Mr. Dahl.)
he was so much offended at them.& on purpose came to a Tavern
Club where he said much.in praise of himself.& at last this
following

An Extempore

I Challange any or all of your Top Tip Top Top-most
Conoisseurs, Proffessors & Judges in the Art of Painting
(besides all pretenders.)

From the Highest to the Lowest, of every degree,
whatsoever
Chafferers bidders & buyers of pictures. their
Bullies Baudes & Panders.
From the Great great. Sr Hu Director & privy Councellor to
Noblemen & Gentlemen that purchase Pictures –
Down to the lowest scrubb even to *Nünis* the Jew all
I do solemnly Challenge & every one of them defy to
compare with me in Judgment & Art –
wittness. *my hand* with sword & Pencil
Given at our *Court*⎫
Club⎭   Aug. 1729'

After his long experience, and his many opportunities, if he took them, of seeing pictures in Europe, Laroon's judgement should have been fairly sound; but the end of the story of Sir Robert's Van Dyck has disappeared as completely as the painting itself – so it can only be assumed that Dahl and Hugh Howard, 'the Great Sr Hu', were right.

This bombastic *Extempore* and his comments about another painting, 'that picture is not worth a penny by Gd. Gd. Dm-me, he knows nothing of the matter',[2] suggest that Vertue was not far wrong in describing Laroon as wanting 'no little conceit of his own capacitys'.[3]

Much information about artists' clubs is to be found in Vertue's notebooks, for he was a frequenter of these gatherings – with a purpose. Here he met and talked with so many artists that he was able to say in 1744 that not many 'Capital Artists' were unknown to him between 1710 and the year in which he was writing; but, as he points out 'the costs or expences to get into companyes conversations Clubbs, has been a continual expence. not sparing the best & most expensive besides the Rose & Crown Clubb so many years and also the Tip top Clubbs of all, for men of the highest Character in Arts & Gentlemen Lovers of Art – calld the Clubb of St. Luke'.[4]

It seems that Laroon's *Extempore* was directed against this 'Tip-top Clubb' – the Society of Virtuosi of St Luke.[5] It was, as Vertue implies, a very respectable body

1 Walpole Society, *Vertue III*, p40.

2 *Ibid.* VI. p34.

3 *Ibid.* III. p65.

4 *Ibid.* p120.

5 British Museum, Add. MS. 39167, *A Folio Tract called the Virtuosi or St Luke's Club.*

with strictly enforced rules against bad behaviour such as cursing and swearing. A special committee of the club was set up to advise collectors on the purchase of pictures, and it may be that Laroon was thought to be trespassing on its preserves. Laroon's own club was the Rose and Crown, which was in existence as early as 1704 when Vertue became a member. Nearly ninety people, including Laroon, who had belonged to or frequented the club during the forty years to 1745, are listed by Vertue, and his description of some of these and of their activities suggests that it was a good deal less reputable than the Club of Virtuosi.[1] The Rosacoronians, as they called themselves, were painted by Smibert in 1724, but this painting has disappeared, only a tiny rough sketch of it by Vertue remaining.[2] There are two other paintings of artists' clubs which probably represent the Rose and Crown. One, in the National Portrait Gallery, by Gawen Hamilton, dated 1735, is described by Vertue as 'the peice of a Conversation of Virtuosis that usually meet at the King's Armes. New bond Street' and contains thirteen named figures.[3] The other, in the Ashmolean Museum, includes six of the same persons – Dahl, Hamilton, Gibbons, Rysbrach, Kent and Bridgeman – and in addition, among others, Vanderbanck and Laroon.[4] If the identifications are accepted, and some are doubtful,[5] the club is unlikely to be St Luke's as Kent and Vanderbanck were not concurrent members: Kent not joining until 1743, four years after the death of Vanderbanck.

As well as these more or less formally constituted clubs, there were many taverns and coffee houses where artists and their friends met, notably 'Old Slaughter's' in St Martin's Lane. Watteau is supposed to have been taken there by his friend and physician Dr Richard Mead, the French Comedians from the Haymarket Theatre used to frequent it and Laroon would have been a likely visitor.

There is no evidence that he took an active part in the theatre after his early appearances, although it has been said that he was 'Harlequin in Rich's company'. This is very unlikely as Rich's pantomimes did not begin until 1716, when Laroon was serving in the army. His movements between the end of his commission in 1718 and the commencement of his new one in 1723 are uncertain; and while it is possible that he returned to the stage during the interval, he does not mention it, nor does his name appear in the very detailed records in the relevant volume of Emmett L. Avery's *The London Stage*, or anywhere else. It seems unlikely, too, that he would play Harlequin, which is an actor-dancer's part, when he was essentially a singer or singer-actor. Confusion over the title of a play *Arlequin Laron, Provost et Juge*, performed by the French Comedians during the years 1718 to 1721, could conceivably be the source of this statement.

That he retained his interest in the theatre is not for one moment in doubt, for apart from the three paintings closely related to, if not actual, theatre scenes, *Dancers and Musicians* [Fig 26], *Scene from Henry the Fourth* [Plate 34] and *Stage Figure* [Plate 36], the pervasive influence of scenic design, of theatrical illustration and of the Italian Comedy on much of his work, is sufficient to show his continuing enthusiasm. He seems also to have had associations with several people active in the theatre world: John James Heidegger, theatre manager and Handel's impresario, who appears in one of Laroon's music party drawings [Plate 24]; Owen MacSwiney, who combined management with a great deal of sometimes very questionable art dealing, whom Laroon had known since 1712, when they were both members of Kneller's Academy, and whose portrait he painted after MacSwiney's return from abroad about 1735; and Stephano Carbonelli, a professional musician, who after

1 Walpole Society, *Vertue VI*, pp31–7.

2 *Ibid.* III, p24.

3 National Portrait Gallery, no. 1384, *A Club of Artists*, 34 x 43 ins. by Gawen Hamilton, 1735.
4 Ashmolean Museum, *A Club of Artists*, 23¾ x 28½ ins.
5 'The figure which is said to be Rysbrach bears so little resemblance to the other portraits of him that it can be assumed that whoever added the numbers and identifications was ignorant of the real identities'. M. I. Webb, *Michael Rysbrach, Sculptor*, 1954, p58.

1 In a list of skilled performers, 'not of the profession of music', J. Hawkins, in *A General History of Music* (1776), 1963 edition, vol. II, p806, refers to Capt. Marcellus Laroon the painter who 'played on the violoncello and composed solos for that instrument'.

2 Horace Walpole, *Correspondence*, edited W. S. Lewis, vol. X, 1941, App. 3, p330.

3 See Cat. No. 125.

4 Walpole Society, *Vertue III*, pp151, 132.

5 Bendall Martyn, *Fourteen Sonatas for Two Violins with a Bass for the Violoncello and a Through Bass for the Harpsichord*, n.d. One of these, in B minor, was broadcast on 18th January, 1958, by the Quatuor Instrumental de Paris. It proved to be a most pleasing piece well worth performing.

6 Versions of the engraving are reproduced in Smith, *Nollekens*, ed. Whitten, Vol. II, opp. p202, and in *The Connoisseur*, vol. LXXV, May 1926, p6. A painting is reproduced in *The Connoisseur*, vol. XVI, November 1906, p188. It is a recurring theme, of which there are other and later versions, the identity of the figures being left, I expect, for the spectator to guess.

leading the orchestras at the Haymarket and Drury Lane theatres, worked with Handel and played for oratorio performances.

As singer, 'cellist and composer,[1] it is to be expected that Laroon would retain his interest, not only in the theatre, but in the musical life of London. His paintings and drawings of musical parties amply demonstrate that he did so. The seventeen-thirties saw the public concert, the music club and the musical conversazione becoming so popular as to affect the theatre, and it has even been said that they were a factor in the failure of Handel's operas in 1731 and 1732, many people preferring the intimacy of music in the home. One of these private music clubs met frequently for some years at the house of Samuel Scott, the marine painter, where its assemblies were graced by Mrs Scott, who is reputed to have been a witty and entertaining woman. Sir Edward Walpole, a member of the club, in a letter written in 1749 to Mrs Scott, humorously professing his passion for her, refers to her 'sitting with your present husband and Mr Marten, who I am told lodges with you, and one of the Walpooles, that people say is forever at your house, and a comical parson, and a watercolour painter' (James Deacon the younger) 'and an engraver of seals for the Mint, and some others I have heard of'.[2] Sir Edward, a capable musician himself, was a patron of Scott's, owning a number of his marine paintings and London views. His brother, Horace, with whom his relations were rather stormy, says that all his 'engageing qualities and talents, formed for splendour and society, were confined to inferior companions, . . . for he was exceedingly passionate, jealous, and impatient of contradiction'.

It is difficult to know when these meetings started but quite possibly early in the thirties, soon after Walpole's return from abroad. All Laroon's music party drawings belong to the years between 1731 and 1736, and unfortunately the one of the Walpole-Scott club which, according to Smith, belonged to James Deacon, has not been found.[3] Deacon, an accomplished musician and Laroon's only known pupil, receives much praise from Vertue: he was 'a genius to Art. well educated in Learning – in Musick & other branches of Gentil Education. a man of strength spirrit & vigour' who 'from a natural genious a curious Eye & a fine hand. draws on vellum & paints, limns in Water colours with great likeness strength – – – an accomplisht musitian such qualifications to such a degree of perfection seldom meet in one person'.[4] The 'Mr Marten' of Sir Edward's letter, was his close friend Bendall Martyn, Secretary of the Excise, who lodged with the Scotts, and who was an admirable musician, a violinist and composer of some published music.[5] It was for Martyn that Laroon made a charming drawing of a musical party in a private house [Fig 55], one of a number of similar studies for various friends, to whom he gave them framed and glazed. The engraver of seals was Richard Yeo, and among 'some others' was Robert Mann, of the Customs House, and Laroon himself, who, 'very engageing in company' was not the least exceptional member of this interesting society.

John Thomas Smith, who provides some information about the Walpole-Scott club, is also responsible for the statement that Laroon was one of 'the three most troublesome and difficult to manage' of Henry Fielding's 'Bow Street visitors' – the other two being 'mad Captain Montagu' and Little Casey, the link boy. Smith reinforces his story, which he quotes as coming from Sanders Welch, Fielding's successor at Bow Street, by stating that Laroon figures in Boitard's print of the *Covent Garden Morning Frolic*.[6] A rather later source of Covent Garden gossip is a little remembered book by John Green, *Odds and Ends about Covent Garden*, where the same character is named Lieutenant King.[1] It may be that Smith had seen the drawing by Laroon, known as *A French Gentn brought at night before the Justice in Bow St* [Plate 31]. Although dated 1740, eight years before Fielding's appointment, it might suggest familiarity with the Bow Street court had it then carried this title. Almost certainly identical with a drawing in Samuel Scott's sale, *A night scene, with figures appearing before a justice* (for which the recently discovered preliminary sketch bears the inscription *Night walkers before a Justice* in Laroon's hand) the present title appears to have been given by Colnaghi's early in the nineteenth century. Although Smith is almost certainly wrong in fact he is probably not far wrong in spirit, as Laroon could hardly be described as an exemplary character.

Laroon's few paintings and drawings of tavern interiors and those of 'Merry Parties', the latter so decorous that the euphemism seems almost justified, give Smith little support; but Vertue's description of the painter with a serving maid at the Rose and Crown Club, leaves no doubt of his intention: 'Capt. Narcissus with feather in his Cap & sword by his side à l'Espagnole meeting the maid who is bringing drink. Catches at her belly, & shows her his Puntle. She looks back & hold one hand before her face . . . Turning to ye Maid, *My dear* let me F. . you'.[2]

It has frequently been asserted that Laroon was a friend and imitator of Hogarth.[3] There is no evidence to support the first, and only misinterpretation of Laroon's work can support the second. It seems inevitable that, moving in the comparatively small circle of London painters, they must have known each other: both were members of the Rose and Crown Club and both friends of Samuel Scott, but there is no evidence of a closer association. Their artistic relationship will be commented on later, but even here there is nothing to suggest intimacy.

Three drawings testify to Laroon's friendship with Matthew Ashton [Plates 11, 12, 6] and one, the caricature of himself and Christian Reisen on horseback [Fig 63], to his friendship with Reisen. From these drawings, Ashton, a minor portrait painter who spent much of his time in Ireland, would appear to have been a convivial soul; in one undoubtedly the butt for a jest.

Much of Laroon's work was done during the thirties and forties – the conversations, the fancy pictures and theatre scenes, and the drawings of the life around him: this, with music, the theatre and the company of his friends seems to have filled his life for some twenty years. His activities after this are less certain. Vertue's last dated mention of him was on 2nd April, 1742, when it was 'his birth day he said – and then enterd the 64. year of his Age'.[4] He is not among the fifty-six painters listed by a writer in 1748 as 'those painters of our nation, now living, many of whom have distinguished themselves and are justly esteemed eminent masters';[5] nor have I found references to him elsewhere. According to Thieme Becker he went, about 1740, to Worcester and then 'back' to York; but no trace of these visits has been found. It is possible that this date should be 1750, and that Laroon spent some of these years in the two cities; but it seems more likely that the statement refers to the times in 1717, 1725 and 1726, when he was stationed at York. A visit to Worcester could very reasonably have been included in his regiment's tour of duty in the latter years.

The portrait of James Macardell [Plate 48], the engraver and a London resident, of 175(?4), suggests that Laroon was still in London in the mid-fifties; but the two *Musical Conversations* [Plates 53, 54], of almost certainly the sixties, are less fashionable and less modish than the earlier conversations, which might point to their having been painted in the provinces. In addition to these, the *Card Players* of 1760 [Plate 52],

1 'John Green' (G. H. Townsend), *Evans Music and Supper Rooms, Odds and Ends about Covent Garden and its Vicinity*, n.d., p6.
Cat No 56

2 Walpole Society, *Vertue VI*, p34 and frontispiece (verso).
3 *Dictionary of National Biography*, 'Laroon'.

Cat Nos 48, 49, 80
Cat No 79

4 Walpole Society, *Vertue III*, p107.

5 W. T. Whitley, *Artists and their Friends in England 1700–1799*, 1928, vol. I, pp103,4, quoting *The Art of Painting*, 1748, by an anonymous writer.

Cat No 8

Cat Nos 27, 28

Cat No 9

1 PCC – Taverner f.221.

2 The Town Clerk and the City Librarian of Oxford have kindly confirmed that the name Laroon does not appear in voters' lists or rate books.

3 A Christopher Yeates was Bailiff of Oxford in 1782 and Mayor in 1792 and 1807. The name Yeates is uncommon and does not appear otherwise in Oxford municipal records. It is tempting and not unreasonable to think that he may be Laroon's Christopher Yeates.

4 *The Daily Advertiser*, 17th and 18th March, 1775. Also with slight variations in *Morning Post and Daily Advertiser*, 16th and 17th March, and *The Gazetteer & New Daily Advertiser*, 16th March.
5 *The Morning Chronicle and London Advertiser*, 4th February, 1778.

6 These portraits by Hals of Thomas Wyck and his wife have not been identified. The only portrait said to be of Wyck that I have been able to trace is attributed to J. C. Verspronck, a photograph of which is in the Witt Library. Professor Seymour Slive has kindly confirmed that no portrait of Wyck by Hals is known to him.

three dated drawings, about a dozen undated paintings and one or two drawings can with confidence be assigned to the fifties and sixties.

In his will,[1] dated 8th August, 1768, he is described as 'of the City of Oxford, heretofore of the Parish of St Paul, Covent Garden' but a codicil made two years later, on 11th June, 1770, uses the expression 'long resident' in the parish of St Mary Magdalen; so it seems likely that some time towards the end of the fifties or early in the sixties he had moved to Oxford. His father's house in Bow Street had passed into other hands in 1704 and as the name Laroon does not appear in the rate books after that date he must have lived in lodgings, as did many other artists and writers in Covent Garden. Likewise in Oxford it is to be supposed as the name is also missing from rate books and voters' lists in that city.[2] He died on 1st June, 1772, in his ninety-fourth year, while still resident in the parish of St Mary Magdalen, in the church of which he was buried.

All we know of his last few years, apart from a number of very lively and characteristic drawings, are the names and pursuits of the friends remembered in his will. He leaves to his servant, Christopher Yeates,[3] to whom he had already given the painting of the Barber's Shop, £200, his linen, wearing apparel, a dozen silver spoons and many of his household goods. To his executors, Richard Combes and William Sandby, he leaves money legacies, to Mrs Elizabeth Long £300 for the purchase of an annuity, and £50 to the poor of the Parish.

All his 'Pictures Prints and Drawings' he left to Gherard Bochman, who died a year later. It seems that Bochman, a painter himself – the 'last surviving disciple of Sir Godfrey Kneller', may not have received the collection as it was sold later in two parts, in 1775 as 'The genuine Collection of Pictures belonging to the late ingenious Captain Laroon',[4] and in 1778 as 'The genuine and valuable Collection of Prints, Books of Prints, and Drawings, of the late ingenious Captain Laroon, well known among the gentleman lovers of the polite arts, for his taste and knowledge in painting . . . many of his own drawings, and a fine old impression of the Luxemburgh Gallery'.[5] These newspaper advertisements are the only evidence we have of the nature of Laroon's collection – no copy of either catalogue has been found – except for Vertue's notes that he owned portraits of Thomas Wyck and his wife by Frans Hals,[6] and of Samuel Barker, the painter, by Vanderbanck. The first of the sale advertisements reads: ' . . . amongst which are the following great Masters, viz. Cuyp, Cap. Laroon, Hobima, Ostade, Kneller, Watteau, Old Laroon, P. Brill, Vangoon, Teniers, Vandevelde, Baptiste, etc. Also a capital Painting purchased out of Mr Fordyce's Collection, and a striking Portrait of Old Laroon, Drawing Master to King William the Third, by himself'. These paintings and the prints and books of prints at the later sale which indicate a rather different kind of collection from those of many artists, where the lots consist for the great part of paintings or drawings by themselves, are of some significance in the consideration of Laroon's own work.

His gregarious instincts do not seem to have deserted him in old age, nor his capacity for enjoyment; and our final picture may be of him playing music with Richard Combes who was to have 'my two violins and my violoncello, and all my Musick Books and Musick papers'; or fishing with Thomas Langford, who was to have his fishing rods and lines; and continuing to exercise the craft of a lifetime with materials bought, perhaps, from his friend, Stephen Fletcher, the stationer in the High Street.

Fig 16 Marcellus Laroon *A Market Tent in Camp* Pencil 11½ × 15⅞ inches
University of London Courtauld Institute of Art

II. METHODS OF WORK AND CHRONOLOGY

Technique and dating

It is more convenient to consider Laroon's technique, signatures and inscriptions, and chronology, before discussing subject matter and the painter's artistic relationships; and, as he was essentially a draughtsman and conceived his paintings, for the most part, as elaborated drawings, to examine the drawings first.

The *Market Tent in Camp* [Fig 16] and the *Execution of Deserters* [Fig 15], both of Cat Nos 37, 38 1707, are the earliest examples of which the dates are fully acceptable, but three small pen and ink sketches of men's heads [Figs 59–61], recently found, seem to antedate them by some years. Stylistically they have resemblances, especially in the treatment of the hands, to Laroon's later work, but technically they resemble more the pen and ink drawings of his father [Fig 11], noticeably in the use of coarse hatching. Two are however clearly signed in Laroon's hand, but not dated, while the inscription on the third begins with the monogram *M*, so often used by Lauron. The style of hat and sleeve ruffle is of the last decade of the seventeenth-century so they are within the span of both father and son. I incline to the view that they are by Laroon when working with or under the immediate influence of his father and that, from the inscription on the third, *Maroon's best Virginia London*, it may be inferred that it is a sketch of Lauron by his son. Still more puzzling is the *Poor Man's Buriall* [Fig 17]. It is apparently authentically inscribed with Laroon's name and the date 1704

Fig 17 Marcellus Lauron *A Poor Man's Burial* Pencil and ink wash 4¾ × 11⅜ inches
Mr & Mrs Paul Mellon

Cat No 77

1 Walpole Society, *Vertue III*, p65.

although the coffin bears a clearly decipherable 1687. Some of the figures, especially the men carrying the coffin, have that lightness of touch which is consistently seen in Laroon's work, but the main body of mourners are heavier and less agile and closer to Lauron's style. The contrast between this drawing and those by Laroon of 1707 [Figs 15, 16] is so great as to make it seem impossible that they are by the same hand, and in spite of the inscription it should perhaps be given to Lauron, although this is not an entirely satisfactory attribution.

Between 1707 and 1770, when Laroon was ninety, I know of only twenty-six drawings which are acceptably both signed and dated: one for each of the years 1718, 19, 20 and 24; eighteen between 1729 and 1748; and one each for 1759, 1762 and 1764. Amongst these a number of undated drawings can, with reasonable assurance, be fitted in. Seventeen, nine of them dated, belong incontrovertibly, wholly or in part, to the last years of his life. The absence of even one firmly attributable drawing to his youth – he was twenty-eight in 1707 – is unfortunate, and unfortunate and remarkable is the absence, except for the two already mentioned, and *Broken on the Wheel* [Plate 2], of drawings made during his many years in the army, for Vertue reports, after briefly summarising his military career, that 'at all these places he often imployd himself to draw or Paint'.[1]

Laroon's usual media were pencil, or pen and ink over pencil with or without wash, and occasionally pencil and red or black chalk. Water-colour wash is used in two but it is difficult to say whether this might not be a later addition. In his late work he always used pen (probably a reed pen) and brown or grey ink, sometimes both, over pencil.

The drawings vary a good deal in the quality of their draughtsmanship and it is plain to see that he never, in a strictly professional sense, made himself completely the master of his pencil. In the earlier examples an occasional lack of dexterity is more than offset by the vigorous line and the spontaneity of movement; but it is where action rather than movement is taking place that deficiencies sometimes reveal themselves as in the dancing man and woman in the *Market Tent* [Fig 16]† or as in the woman throwing the stocking in the otherwise masterly *Wedding Night* [Plate 32]†.

By 1718, the date of the sketch portrait of *John Rollos* [Fig 53]† he had developed to the full the light, flickering, rococo line which makes his drawings of the twenties and thirties so alive. The *Alms men* of 1720 [Fig 38]† and the *Frenchman at Bow Street* of 1740 [Plate 31]†, both derived from the life, are very fine indeed. The latter, an assembly of twenty-seven people almost all in action, intricately arranged in the space of a small room, presented a formidable task even to a highly accomplished draughts-man and might well be compared with Hogarth's finished drawing for plate ten of *Industry and Idleness* [Fig 18].

The *Music Party (Va)* of 1736 [Plate 24]†, in pen over pencil with Indian ink wash delicately used, is one of those works which Laroon himself described as 'finished'. Comparison with the sketch [Plate 25]† shows that the finished drawing has lost nothing in spontaneity and vigour; in fact the tightening-up of the grouping has added to these qualities. *Promenade in the Mall* of 1744 [Plate 37] begins to show perhaps some slight loss of concentration and firmness – which is noticeable in the *Woodman* [Plate 41] of four years later and much more so in the *Countryman and Appleseller* of 1764 [Fig 56], where the flickering line has become flaccid. But the liveliness of the sketch of *Lovers in a Glade* dated 1759 [Plate 50] suggests that one should allow for the in-consistencies of age – he was, after all, eighty in this year. How felicitously in his earlier years he could use red chalk is shown by the masterly study of a Birdcatcher of probably the mid-thirties [Plate 27].

The splendid drawings which Laroon made when he was over ninety come however as a surprise. Underlying the short, broken and slightly tremulous pen work, an exaggeration of the earlier flickering line, is sometimes a firmer pencil line, suggesting that some of these are unfinished sketches completed several, perhaps many, years after they were begun. The architectural features remain in pencil with the main lines of the buildings drawn with a ruler, which give a sense of stability to these otherwise quite exuberant drawings.

Except for five the dates can be accepted as reasonably reliable but are always a little open to question, owing to what I believe to have been a frequent habit of Laroon's, of inscribing, signing and dating not at the time of production. Of the five, the *Dutchman and his Wife* [Plate 16] has signature and date, 1702, in Laroon's hand but pencilled over. Stylistically it is later than 1702 and although it is difficult to date the costume accurately neither the man nor the woman is wearing Dutch or English clothes of the beginning of the century. Much the same can be said of the *Ancient Couple* [Plate 17] although the considerable element of caricature makes it even more difficult to assess. Drawings with false dates are the *Scene in a Garden* [Plate 15] and the *Rocky Landscape with figures* [Plate 38], the *1732* of the former having been altered to *1702* and the *1743* of the latter to *1703;* and the *Horseman and Beggar* [Plate 57], clearly later than is implied by the inked over *1732*, which should, I think, be *1762*. One drawing has a false signature *W. Hogarth* most inexpertly forged over the original, partly deleted, *M. Laroon*. The date *1729* appears unaltered and is con-sistent with its style.

Five paintings only are firmly dated: one each for the years 1731, 1735, 1740, 1742,

Fig 18 William Hogarth *The Industrious 'Prentice Alderman of London, the Idle one Brought before him and Impeached by his Accomplice*
Pen, ink and grey wash
9⅛ × 15⅜ inches
British Museum

†Cat Nos 37, 94, 39, 41, 56, 55, 85

Cat No 58

Cat No 7

Cat No 63

Cat No 61

Cat No 91

Cat No 82

Cat No 83
Cat No 47
Cat No 57
Cat No 98

and 1746. One is acceptably dated 175(?4) and one has a probably authentic 1760 on the back of the canvas. Two others can be acceptably dated from related drawings, one as 1725 and one as 1748.

Laroon's painting technique seems to have remained basically unaltered. As his earliest known painting, the *Musical Assembly* [Plate 3] can be reasonably dated between 1715 and 1720, when he was already approaching forty and after he had resumed his work at Kneller's Academy, it is difficult to know whether his use of a greyish-brown or greenish-brown ground derives from the early days of his father's tuition or from this later time. Thomas Bardwell, writing in 1756, reminds us that Kneller, after Lely's death, fell into what he calls a 'slighter manner' of laying a ground 'and invented the cold grey-coloured Cloths, on which he established his slight expeditious manner'[1] – a description which could well be applied to Laroon's work. This kind of cold ground is quite consistent in all the known paintings. On it he drew the outlines in brown and then filled in with colour. An excellent example of his method is to be seen on the easel in the *Self portrait* [Fig 14], where on the grey-brown ground the head and features are drawn in brown and a little red has been applied to the nostrils.

The *Lovers in a Glade* [Fig 19], of 1731, has paint thick enough to be opaque, and shows some feeling for texture and surface, but in the *Village Wedding* [Plate 19], of five years later, one is becoming more aware of the linear and less of the painterly element, and Laroon is beginning to use oils more like a water-colour wash. It is presumably to paintings of this kind that Vertue is alluding in 1740 '– other peices of Conversations. well designd. – the compositions remarkable & Varyed. tho not so well colourd. with a body of Colours. – they seem rather like drawings colourd with transparent colours all over too much alike – but have a good effect'.[2] The linear quality becomes more marked and comparison of two very similar scenes, the *Tavern Interior* of 1742 [Plate 35] and the *Card Players* of 1760 [Plate 52] shows how, in the latter the figures have become outlines filled in with colour, chiaroscuro has disappeared and the highlights have been emphasised by brush points of white.

Within the framework provided by these dated or dateable paintings it is not easy to fit convincingly some of the other works. Those which I find most difficult to place are the two musical conversations [Plates 53, 54] and the figures on horseback [Plates 55, 58] where brush-point highlights are so prominent. While this kind of highlight can be seen as early as the *Musical Assembly* [Plate 3] and as late as the 1760 *Card Players* [Plate 52] I think that these paintings must belong to a fairly circumscribed period. That this feature is not mentioned by Vertue in 1740 when he had clearly looked critically at Laroon's technique, and that it is not very noticeable in the 1742 *Tavern Interior* [Plate 35] nor in the *Woodman* of 1748 [Plate 41], suggest a date after this. For this and other reasons to be mentioned later, I have assigned this group of works to the sixties.

I have found it difficult also to date the painting *The Lovers in a Park* [Fig 31]. Since I saw it some years ago it has been cleaned and this has served to emphasize the impasto of the highlights – not yet of the brush-point kind but approaching it. Painted when Laroon was at the height of his powers it is one of his most delicate works with the wash-like paint and the subtle red shadows in the man's black clothes. I should now put it as some ten years later than my former suggestion of 1735.[3] It is clearly unwise to suppose too cut-and-dried a 'development' in a non-professional painter who worked in fits and starts for his own pleasure and amusement. With this proviso

Cat No 10

1 T. Bardwell, *The Practice of Painting – ,* 1756, p5.

Cat No 11

Cat No 2
Cat No 3

2 Walpole Society, *Vertue III*, p100.

Cat Nos 5, 9

Cat Nos 27, 28
Cat Nos 30–33
Cat No 10
Cat No 9

Cat Nos 5, 7

Cat No 19

3 R. Raines, 'Marcellus Laroon the Younger II', *Connoisseur Year Book*, 1959, p116.

in mind Laroon's manner can be seen as gradually changing from painterly to linear with the paint becoming thinner and thinner except for the impasted highlights.

While there are several preliminary sketches for drawings only two sketches for paintings are known, those for the *Dinner Party* [Plate 5] and the *Woodman* [Plate 41]. They suggest that Laroon used sketches as a means for determining the general composition and that revision of figure grouping and surroundings and detailed consideration of individual figures were left until he was working on the canvas. I know of no sketch for a single figure in a painting although a study for two figures in the *Levee* is said to exist. Thus it appears that Laroon's method of composition was akin to Hogarth's and not to Watteau's.

Cat Nos 1,7

Signatures and Inscriptions

Laroon signed his drawings <u>M</u>, *Mar*, or *Marcellus*, *Laroon* and except in one added *Fecit*, *fecit* or *F*. Two are initialled *M.L.F.* and one has *M. Lar. F.* Two have the word *Dux* between *Laroon* and *Fecit* and three late drawings have, before the signature, *Aetatis* or *Aetat* 92.

On the five signed and dated paintings are *M. Laroon. 1731*, *Marcellus Laroon. F.1735*, *Mar. Laroon. 1740*, *M. Laroon F.1742* and *Mar. Laroon. F1746*. The inscription on the *Card Players* appears to have been repainted *Marcellus Larroon Invenit & pinxit 1760 Anno Aetatis 80*. The portrait of *James Macardell* is not signed on the front of the canvas but was inscribed on the back in black paint in Laroon's, or a very similar, hand *James Maca – | Marcellus Laroon 175(?4)*.

Provenances

The original owners of few of Laroon's works are known. Only one painting, the *Dinner Party* [Plate 5], in the Royal Collection, remains in original ownership. Christopher Yeates, his servant, was the first owner of the *Barber's Shop* [Plate 59]. Of the drawings, in the eighteenth-century two belonged to Samuel Scott, three to Horace Walpole, two to Mathew Ashton and one each to Bendall Martyn, Stephano Carbonelli and Edmund Prideaux. Three now in the Ashmolean Museum were in the collection of Francis Douce. With these exceptions it has proved impossible to trace any with certainty beyond the nineteenth-century and many beyond the twentieth. This can no doubt be explained by the very small value attached to works by Laroon in the eighteenth and nineteenth centuries: a painting of a conversation fetching two pounds, seven shillings in 1753[1] and fifteen drawings selling for eight shillings in 1810.[2] Indeed as late as 1934 the *Musical Assembly* was bought at auction for twenty-nine pounds. Other works sold during the present century and until the last few years, have fetched derisory sums or have been bought in.

Cat No 1
Cat No 34

1 Lord Orford's sale, 1753, second day (8).

2 Thomas Kirgate's sale, December 1810, fourth day (91).

Fig 19 Marcellus Laroon *Lovers in a Glade I* Oil on canvas 16½ × 13⅛ inches
Collection unknown

III WORKS

The death of Louis Laguerre in 1721 and of Sir Godfrey Kneller two years later marked the end of the overt Franco-Italian domination of decorative painting in this country and of the Netherlandish-German domination of portraiture. But during the whole of the century foreign influences, more subtle and less tangible or definable were to play an important, even a vital, part in the development of painting in Britain. The long-term residence here of lesser foreign painters who became absorbed into English life; the short-term visits of more important figures; and the increasing familiarity with contemporary and near-contemporary European work through the wider dissemination of engravings, were all of consequence. The changing fashion in the valuation of Italian, Dutch and French art is fascinatingly revealed in comments by observers of the scene and even more specifically in the sale catalogues of the period.

Study of a painter such as Laroon, who was of independent means and had no need to follow the fashionable trend, may serve to show how powerful this trend can be in the world of the arts. Taught by his father, he would be especially familiar with the low-life scenes by him and by Egbert van Heemskerck the elder, which can be regarded as the ignoble epitaph to the seventeenth-century association of England and the Netherlands. He would also be aware, if not in 1712 when he worked in Kneller's Academy, at least during the twenties, of the re-orientation of taste from Dutch towards French and Italian art.

James Thornhill in his 1711 diary of travels mentions only a few Dutch painters, writes much more about the buildings, and sketches many architectural features. He finds Flemish painting of greater interest, except Van Eyck, whose altarpiece of the Lamb was, to Thornhill's baroque taste, 'but moderate'.[1] By 1727 the position was such that George Berkeley, in explaining why some pictures which Prior had sent to auction had fetched only forty-five pounds, writes: 'The truth of it is, that of late years the taste lies so much towards Italian pictures, many of which are daily imported, that Dutch pictures go off but heavily. Mr Smibert did not think they would have brought so much'.[2] And the last word must rest with Richard Graham who, in 1716, says of Rembrandt: 'He died Anno 1668; for nothing more to be admir'd, than for having heap'd up a noble Treasure of Italian *Prints* and *Drawings*, and for making no better use of them'.[3] Frank Simpson's study of sale catalogues, 'Dutch Paintings in England before 1760', shows how the interest in Dutch painting again began to grow during the early seventeen forties.[4]

The arrival in London of Watteau in 1719 for a short stay; of Philip Mercier about 1725 for the rest of his life; of Gravelot in 1732; the presence since the early seventeen-

1 J. Thornhill, *Diary of a journey from London – – – to Holland from 21 May to 19 June, 1711 – – –*, British Museum, Add.MS. 34, 788. This is a copy of the original MS. which is in the Victoria and Albert Museum.
2 G. Berkeley, *Works of – – –*, vol. 8, 1956, *Letters*, ed. A. A. Luce, p177, letter 123. The 'Mr Smibert' is John Smibert (1684–1751) a Scottish painter who accompanied Berkeley to Bermuda in 1728 and then settled in Boston, U.S.A. where he established a flourishing practice as a portrait painter.
3 R. Graham, *A Short Account of the most Eminent Painters* appended to Du Fresnoy, *The Art of Painting*, 2nd edition, 1716, p372. The note on Rembrandt is not in the first edition of 1695.
4 F. Simpson, 'Dutch Paintings in England before 1760', *Burlington Magazine*, vol. 95, February 1953, pp39–42.

twenties, of a number of French engravers; and the publication of engravings after Watteau, culminating with the *Recueil Jullienne* in 1735, were all significant in the approach towards French rococo art.

Laroon was aware of Watteau at least as early as 1720, as the 'cello leaning against a stool in the *Musical Assembly* is surely borrowed directly from *Les Charmes de la Vie*; so it appears that he anticipated rather than followed the general trend towards French art. It may be that the part played by Gravelot has been over-estimated; at least it seems certain that Laroon completed one of his most French pictures, the *Lovers in a Glade* [Fig 19], in 1731, the year before Gravelot came to England. It is interesting to see then how five years later in the *Village Wedding* [Plate 19] Dutch-Flemish elements are prominent and how, by 1742, he is painting a full-blown Teniers subject – the *Tavern Scene*. How French rococo art, Dutch-Flemish low-life subjects, book illustration, the theatre, and the work of Veronese and perhaps of Marco Ricci influenced Laroon's observation of the life around him will be considered in some detail as we look at his work in the following sections.

He was predominantly a painter of invented scenes, of pictures of imagination and fancy; and there is an ill-defined division between these fancy pictures, his conversation pieces, stage scenes and paintings of genre subjects. Although I have separated his work, for convenience of discussion, into Fancy pictures, Stage scenes and related compositions, Portraits, Conversation pieces, and Genre and caricature, these categories are more than a little arbitrary because it is often impossible to say whether a particular painting should be regarded as a true conversation piece or as a fancy picture; or whether a portrait head is a true portrait or perhaps the head of a model.

'Conversation' or 'Conversation Piece' was not specifically applied in the early eighteenth-century to that kind of picture which we now mean by the term – small portrait groups in an intimate setting with identifiable people taking part in some usually non-utilitarian activity. Buckeridge's comment in 1706 that Lauron was 'fam'd for pictures in Little, commonly called Conversation-Pieces' almost certainly refers to genre in the Dutch manner. It seems however that the term with its present meaning was coming into use during the 1760s, Romney for instance exhibiting 'A conversation (portraits of his brothers . . . figures are about two and a half feet)' in 1766[1] and Francis Cotes 'A conversation' two years later.[2] Horace Walpole was still using the term with its seventeenth-century meaning as late as 1786 when he wrote of Terborch as 'a Dutch painter of conversation' but an advertisement by an itinerant painter in 1795 'small portraits in Oil, at *One Guinea* each: Conversation pieces in proportion'[3] implies that by this date it was the accepted term, even in the provinces, for the small portrait group.

The genesis and history of the conversation piece has been traced by several writers, most recently and in most detail, by Mr Ralph Edwards in his '*Early Conversation Pictures*', with, as his starting-point, Van Eyck's *Arnolfini and his Wife*; through Dutch and Flemish seventeenth and early eighteenth-century painters – Molenaer, Metsu, Jacob van Oost, Gonzales Coques and Nicholaas Verkolje; the Frenchmen, especially Robert Tournières, and of course Watteau, whose *La Conversation* holds an important place; all providing a line of descent, if an indirect one.

But in no painting by Laroon do we know the identity of the sitters or the setting with sufficient certainty to say that it is a true conversation. There is indeed frequent precedent for paintings of this indeterminate kind and the confusion inherent in these

1 Free Society of Artists, 1766 (144).
2 Society of Artists of Great Britain, 1768 (31).

3 *Hull Advertiser*, 8 August 1795.

Cat No 2

works is exemplified in, for example, Jan Steen's *Delft Burgomaster*[1] where the Burgomaster, sitting outside his house and accompanied by his daughter, both apparently portraits, is attending to the business of a poor woman with a little boy, who might both have come straight from one of Steen's genre scenes, such as the *Grace before meat*[2]. It was also a habit of Steen's to introduce portraits, often of himself and his family, into what seem to be otherwise pure genre pictures. If we turn from Holland to France we find Watteau introducing portraits into fantasias. Examples of this are Sirois in *Sous un habit de Mezzetin*[3] and Wleughels in *Les Charmes de la Vie*[4]. Laroon continued this custom, his conversation pieces verging on the fancy pictures and vice-versa – equivalents almost of the landscape capricci of the vedutiste.

Fancy Pictures

Certain subjects, a man and a woman in a woodland glade, or one or two riders perhaps with a beggar asking for alms, are among Laroon's favourite themes. Some appear to be straight-forward genre while others, having more than a touch of fancy, carry allusions to the theatre. The subject of Laroon's *Lovers in a Glade I* was much used by Watteau and other eighteenth-century French painters; for instance in Watteau's *Les Agrémens de L'esté* [Fig 20] the engraving of which was published in the same year as Laroon's painting, and in a number of works by Jean-François Detroy, whose *La Surprise*[5] is a variant of the theme. It was to be continued in England by Francis Hayman and in Holland by Cornelis Troost [Fig 21]. Although Laroon's painting is originally conceived it shows unequivocally the French influence, and must be the first scene painted in England by an English-born artist to show some real appreciation of the rococo aspect of French art. It suggests closer acquaintance with it than the study of engravings alone would provide. But however close the resemblance may be it is unusual to detect in Laroon's work a frank borrowing; unlike Philip Mercier, some of whose figures are taken almost literally from Watteau, notably that of a seated woman from *Fêtes Venitiennes* which he uses no less than three times in his work.

The *Lovers in a Glade*, and Laroon's other predominantly French-influenced pictures, the *Commedia dell' Arte scene* [Fig 28]† and the *Fête Galante* [Plate 20]†, retain a certain naive quality which is far from unattractive. Not quite everything is related to the rococo rhythm, figures are slightly regimented and it can perhaps be said that, in crossing the Channel, the rococo, while retaining its general pattern, tended to lose some of its rhythm. Mercier, to mention him yet again, soon after coming to this country in about 1725, as a follower and imitator of Watteau, painted the *Tyrconnel Family*, which shows this rhythmic jerkiness. Even Hogarth at his most rococo, in the enchanting *Indian Emperor*, the second scene from *Marriage-à-la-Mode* and the *Strolling Actresses dressing in a Barn* is not without it. One is reminded, if it is legitimate to draw a literary parallel, of Pope's *Dunciad*:

> To isles of fragrance, lily-silver'd vales,
> Diffusing langour in the painting gales;
> To lands of singing or of dancing slaves,
> Love-whispering woods, and lute-resounding waves.

Divorced from its context, it evokes the very theme of Watteau's *Embarquement pour Cythère*, but how far from the rococo is the rhythmic regularity of the heroic couplet.

It was, I think, Borenius who first drew attention to Laroon's dependence on Watteau, and who also saw Laroon 'in his handling of paint, particularly in his trees'

1 Coll. Lady Janet Douglas-Pennant.

2 National Gallery, London.

3 Wallace Collection.
4 Wallace Collection.
5 Victoria and Albert Museum.

Fig 20 Antoine Watteau (after)
Les Agrémens de l'esté (detail)
Engraving by Jacques de Favannes

Fig 21 Cornelis Troost *A man and woman in a landscape* (detail) Indian ink with grey wash $9\frac{3}{4} \times 12\frac{3}{16}$ inches
Fodor Collection, Amsterdam

†Cat Nos 15, 14

Fig 22 William Hogarth *Before* Oil on canvas 14 × 17½ inches
Fitzwilliam Museum, Cambridge

1 T. Borenius, 'The Kaleidoscope of Taste',
The Studio, December, 1931, p356.

Cat No 3

as a possible influence on Gainsborough.[1] One might see in the *Lovers in a Glade*, and in some of his other figures in landscapes, a French-inspired influenced on Gainsborough, in addition to that of Gravelot, who did not arrive in England until the year after Laroon had painted this picture. It is also of interest because of the contrast with a similar scene by Hogarth who, in 1730 and into 1731, was painting the two sets of *Before* and *After*: the indoor scenes where the tale of seduction is told without any of the graces, and the outdoor scenes where the *Before* [Fig 22] has a caricatured elegance. Although superficially alike in composition and in the handling of the wooded background, comparison points the difference between the mildly erotic grace of Laroon's scenic painting and the Frenchified quality of Hogarth's very English narrative picture.

The painting which I regard as Laroon's masterpiece, the *Village Wedding* of 1735 [Fig 23], is of an evening scene painted in browns and greens with subtly placed touches of colour: the girl on the left in pink, the woman riding pillion in blue with a pink cap-ribbon, and the lady in pale blue with her page leading the horse. The subject is far from explicit but seems perhaps to have been suggested by a group of figures on the extreme right of the engraving by N. de Larmessin of *L'Accordée de Village* [Fig 24], one of Watteau's last pictures to be engraved – in 1735, the year when the *Oeuvre gravé* was published. The many figures in procession, some so insubstantial as to be uncountable, making their way through and down the sides of a

Fig 23 Marcellus Laroon *The Village Wedding* (detail of plate 19)
Private Collection, England

Fig 24 Antoine Watteau (after) *L'Accordée de Village* (detail)
Engraving by Nicolas de Larmessin

rocky defile, is a highly original concept. I know of no other painting of a similar subject, although it has been regarded as a rural and bucolic version of *L'Embarquement pour Cythère*.[1] Many of the more substantial figures are of surprising individuality and recall Teniers. The debt, to the Low Countries is, in fact, greater than the debt to France; with Rubens' *Kermesse* not far away. Notably successful is the spatial composition, which in much of Laroon's work is not his strongest point.

But whatever the significance of this scene may be, it is here that the painter has achieved a synthesis of his own acute observation with the rococo of Watteau and the low-life painting of the Netherlands. Throughout Laroon's work these last conflict and merge: the poetry with the prose; the evocation of Utopia with the facts of life; and only occasionally are they blended sufficiently to allow us to forget the derivations. Had he been able more often to parallel his achievement in the *Village Wedding*, he would rank as something more than a little master.

Equally tantalising in their lack of explicitness are the so-called *Black Prince* [Plate 33] and the *Woodman* [Plate 41]. The *Black Prince*, aptly described as an early 'Gothick' picture, is quite firmly painted, although the beautiful range of greens in the foliage has a light, almost sketchy effect. In a clearing in a dense wood a mounted figure in armour is dramatically motioning to an attendant dressed like a Cromwellian pikeman. The title of the *Black Prince* has been retained for convenience of reference although the scene seems to have no connection with that historical figure.

1 Louvre, and Staatliche Museen, Berlin–Dahlem.

Cat Nos 17, 7

It is a forerunner of the typical later eighteenth-century illustration of a scene from an early romance – perhaps from *Arcadia* or, if the rather delicate figure in armour is a woman, she might be Britomart from *The Faerie Queen* or Bradamante from *Orlando Furioso*.

I do not recognise the subject of the *Woodman* as illustrating a scene from a novel or from a play. The change in detail, from the background figure of a woman and a boy picking apples in the drawing to a young woman nursing a baby in the painting, suggests rather that it is a fancy picture. Even the woodman's action is ambiguous: is he pointing the way or threatening as the young man's protective gesture might suggest? The compositional changes are however all to the good and the painting is more nicely balanced than the drawing. The placing of the figures against a sunset sky has a delicacy and a subtlety which is infrequent in English painting before Gainsborough and which one meets unexpectedly in many of Laroon's works. There is too a charming sense of colour harmony: against a background, except for the sunset, of low toned greens and browns, he wears a grey coat and she a dull gold dress and hat; small colour accents – the basket of fruit and the woman's red shoes – suffice to throw the figures into relief.

The equally beautiful painting, here entitled *Fête Galante*, which Borenius reproduced in his appreciative note on Laroon in 1931 as *Conversation Piece* [Plate 20], has since been destroyed. Like the *Commedia dell' Arte Scene* [Fig 28], it is repeatedly reminiscent of Watteau, the dependence being both in mood and motif: the exquisite young woman on the extreme left, the player of the arch-lute and the singing woman with basket of fruit might almost have come direct from *L'Amour au théâtre Français*, but one searches Watteau for them and fails to find them. And the idyllic atmosphere is disturbed by the intrusion of satire in the incident on the right where the fat, elderly and very ugly woman's hand is being sycophantically kissed by the kneeling young man – an incident perhaps in another rake's progress.

Stage scenes and related compositions.

Mention has already been made of Laroon's early stage experiences, of his friendship with people in the world of the theatre and of a possible link with Marco Ricci who was employed as a stage designer. Settings and backgrounds in some of Laroon's paintings have been seen as resembling tapestry but to me they are much more reminiscent of stage scenery. The affinity between certain features in the paintings now to be considered and some of those in the fancy pictures needs no stressing.

The *Scene from Henry the Fourth, Part I* of 1746 [Fig 25a, Plate 34],† convincingly naturalistic, represents a moment in an actual stage performance. Falstaff is here, in Act III Scene III, gibing at Bardolph, whom Laroon paints with a fiery face and carbuncular nose – 'Do thou amend thy face, or I'll amend my life: thou art our Admiral, thou bearest the lantern in the poop, but 'tis in the nose of thee: thou art the Knight of the Burning Lamp'; and a few lines later, not to be outdone, he replies to Bardolph's remark that ' 'Sblood, I would my face were in your belly' with 'God-a-mercy, so should I be sure to be heart-burn'd'. It is at this moment that Mistress Quickly enters and she is here shown on a very arbitrary staircase which seems to come from nowhere. The rail-like structure on which are flagon and glass, and the very odd property on the right which resembles, but can hardly be a fireplace, free-standing as it is, are equally illogical and suggest that this is a painting based on a particular performance but not an accurate record of it: a compression of a stage

Cat No 14
Cat No 15

† Cat No 6

Fig 25a Marcellus Laroon
James Quin (?) as Falstaff
(detail from *Scene from Henry the Fourth, Part I*)
Mr & Mrs Paul Mellon

scene within the spatial limits of an upright picture.

Examination of the figures reveals two further apparent anomalies: the discrepancies in the characterisation and in the costumes of Falstaff and Bardolph. Bardolph is typically Laroon and yet a convincing Bardolph, but Falstaff is facially un-Falstaffian in terms of either Shakespeare or Laroon. For this reason I think that Falstaff is intended to be a portrait: a portrait in fact of James Quin who played the role, which he had made very much his own, at Covent Garden on 6th December 1746 and at several performances later in the month. Allowing for the inevitable difficulties in comparing straight and character portraits, by different hands in different media, there are, I suggest, acceptable similarities between this figure and Hogarth's portrait of Quin [Fig 25b] of about the same date,[1] Gainsborough's portrait of some fifteen years later[2] [Fig 25c] and Macardell's mezzotint.

As regards costume Bardolph is in contemporary dress but Falstaff wears a Tudor-like cap and ruff, a Van Dyck jerkin, high boots and an eighteenth-century coat used as a cloak. In his *Shakespeare from Betterton to Irving* G.C.D. Odell points out that there was little more attempt at historical accuracy in the dressing of plays in the time of Cibber, and even of Garrick, than in that of Betterton, but that one of the few exceptions seems always to have been Falstaff 'who undoubtedly continued to wear something like the costume fastened upon him in Shakespeare's day – the high boots, loosely falling to the knee, the jerkin with points, the round hat with a feather – – – and I am inclined to think that Dame Quickly was unique among the women in being differentiated by a peaked Elizabethan hat'.[3]

Odell's view that Falstaff and the Hostess were traditionally costumed in eighteenth-century performances is amply confirmed by contemporary paintings and drawings, and now additionally by this Laroon picture; but Hogarth and Hayman painted scenes in which Falstaff's companions as well are dressed in costumes intended to be of the period.[4]

Whether 'historical' costume in theatrical paintings was a record of contemporary stage practice, or the result of artistic license, might be considered in the light of Moelwyn Merchant's discussion of the varying kinds of 'theatricality' in early eighteenth-century illustrations to Shakespeare, especially in Rowe's editions of 1709 and 1714. 'Where', he writes, 'the plates are unambiguously influenced by stage practice there is a mixed derivation from the contemporary theatre, from operatic and masque convention, and when the play was rarely performed, from conventions of a much earlier period'.[5] But he suggests that 'stage influence' does not necessarily mean recollections of stage performances, and that some of the effects shown in the illustrations would not have been obtainable on the stages of the period. Merchant's views are applicable also to some of Laroon's less easily definable stage and stage-influenced pictures.

The *Dancers and Musicians* [Fig 26], which has decidedly the feel of an actual stage scene, is equally interesting but less explicit than the *Falstaff*. On a shallow and narrow stage a young man and a young woman dance to the music of a violin-playing Harlequin and a double-bass player in black, who stand on plinths on each side, while a Punch-like face peers over the back-screen. The shape of what appears to be the proscenium opening suggests that the dance is taking place on an inner stage such as is shown in two engraved plates in the 1741 edition of Gherardi's *Le Théâtre Italien* for *La Coquette*, and still more convincingly for *Les Souhaits* [Fig 27], where Harlequin and Columbine dance between two Muses standing on plinths. In these

Fig 25b William Hogarth
James Quin (detail)
Tate Gallery, London

Fig 25c Thomas Gainsborough
James Quin (detail)
National Gallery of Ireland, Dublin

Cat No 26

1 National Gallery, London, no. 1935.
2 National Gallery of Ireland, Dublin, no.565.
3 G. C. D. Odell, *Shakespeare from Betterton to Irving*, 1921, vol. 1. pp204–5.
4 Hogarth's *Falstaff reviewing his troops*, painting in the collection of the Earl of Iveagh, drawing at Windsor Castle; Hayman's painting of the same scene, in the National Gallery of Ireland, no 295.
5 M. Merchant, *Shakespeare and the Artist*, 1959, p49 note 3 and p50.

Fig 27 Unknown artist Frontispiece to
Les Souhaits in Gerhardi *Le Théâtre
Italien*, 1741

Fig 26 Marcellus Laroon *Dancers and Musicians* Oil on canvas $34\frac{1}{2} \times 27\frac{1}{4}$ inches
Private Collection, England

Cat No 15

the main stage clearly continues forward but in the Laroon painting this arrangement
is not apparent. I know of no other evidence of the use of this kind of inner stage, and
other possibilities are that the entertainment is taking place on a small stage at one
of the London Fairs, or even in a private house.

The *Commedia dell' Arte Scene* of about 1735 [Fig 28], is, if not unique, one of very
few Italian-comedy pictures painted in England in the mid-eighteenth century.

Fig 28 Marcellus Laroon *Commedia dell' Arte Scene* Oil on canvas 36¼ × 34½ inches Mr & Mrs Paul Mellon

1 *Comedians at a Fountain* at Windsor Castle (O. Millar, *Tudor, Stuart, and Early Georgian Pictures in the Royal Collection*, 1963, no. 524, pl. 194) and two *Fêtes Galantes*, with the Newhouse Gallery, New York, in 1951, (one reproduced in R. Rey, *Quelques satellites de Watteau*, 1931, pl. 11), are almost certainly by Mercier.

2 W. Hogarth, *The Analysis of Beauty*, ed. J. Burke, 1955, pp158–9.
3 H. Adhémar, *Watteau*, 1950, reproduces the painting as plate 57.

Fig 29 Antoine Watteau (after) *La Cascade*
Engraving by G. Scotin
† Cat No 19

Fig 30 Philippe Mercier *La Promenade*
Oil on canvas 14½ × 12 inches

Apart from Laroon only Philip Mercier seems to have painted Commedia scenes and then only when he was under the influence of Watteau.[1] Later he did no more than introduce an occasional unconvincing Pierrot into a fancy picture. Harlequin, and less frequently Scaramouche, Pantaloon and other characters appear however in English caricature and satire, usually in direct criticism of this form of entertainment which, in the first half of the eighteenth-century, had such a considerable effect on the lighter English stage. A number of prints, including *Masquerades and Operas* and *A Just View of the English Stage* by Hogarth, and others by his contemporaries, witness the unwelcome infiltration of the theatre by this lively and bawdy entertainment. Nevertheless, although Hogarth painted no Commedia scenes and used prints to satirize the players and their plays, he wrote a sensitively appreciative description of the dance movements of some of the characters in *The Analysis of Beauty*.[2]

The Commedia characters in Laroon's painting are Scaramouche playing a guitar on the extreme left; two innamorati in the centre, he in pink, she in blue; Pierrot; and in front of him the Doctor with an innamorata or a courtesan – a figure perhaps too richly dressed for Columbine; and Harlequin playing a violin and perching on the shoulders of a scowling Hercules. While there are no direct borrowings the influence of Watteau is manifest. These Commedia figures are much more akin to Watteau's graphic *Comédie Italien* than to the characters of the true Italian comedies as depicted in sixteenth-century paintings and engravings, or to the seventeenth-century engravings of Callot and the paintings of Jan Steen.

Of the other figures, the two of indeterminate sex in long robes seated at the back, and the little fat man next to Pierrot, are curiously out-of-place and inexplicit, until one realises that this is probably an imaginative scene based on one of the Commedia entertainments which became so popular in the London theatre, after their introduction by the French comedians who played at the Little Theatre in the Haymarket intermittently between 1718 and 1735. The lists of diverse characters taking part in these are more than enough to explain the appearance of any unlikely figure. The cast of *Harlequin Orpheus or the Magical Pipe*, at Drury Lane on 3rd March, 1734/5, *A New Grotesque Pantomime Entertainment*, included Apollo, Mercury and Caliope; Harlequin, Pierrot and Columbine; Country Squire, Farmer and Inn-keeper; and two years earlier, *Apollo and Daphne* had, besides the title roles, Harlequin, Scaramouche, Columbine, Burgomaster and Boor Servant. The highly sophisticated twentieth-century equivalent is the Strauss-Hofmannsthal *Ariadne auf Naxos*, which, according to Hofmannsthal, was 'actually distilled from the two theatrical elements of Molière's age: from the mythological opera and from the *maschere*, the dancing and singing comedians' and which 'Callot might have drawn'.

Watteau's painting of two people standing in a park, *La Cascade* [Fig 29][3] was imitated by Mercier in *La Promenade* [Fig 30] and by Lancret; but while in both versions the dresses and the background were altered the composition remained entirely Watteau's. Laroon's *Lovers in a Park* [Fig 31]† has no such direct ancestry and yet is quite close to Watteau, several of whose figures could have served as Laroon's starting point. Painted very lightly with that flickering touch which he used so effectively, it shows two people in fancy dress – he in black with red-lined cloak, she in white and puce-pink – walking forwards as if to the front of a stage. The background has some sense of depth but a most emphatic decorative pattern and might well be a backcloth, the whole scene being reminiscent of the theatre. It is of considerable interest in the light of Moelwyn Merchant's previously quoted remarks

Fig 31 Marcellus Laroon *Lovers in a Park* Oil on canvas 24½ × 20¼ inches
Mr & Mrs Paul Mellon

Fig 32 Unknown artist Frontispiece for
As You Like It, Rowe, 1709
Engraving

† Cat No 20
† Cat No 11

1 The present whereabouts of this painting is
unknown but there is a photograph in the
Witt Library.
2 Walpole Society, *Vertue III*, p65.
3 *Ibid*. p100.

Fig 33 Marcellus Laroon
Self-Portrait
(see also Figure 14)

to compare Laroon's painting, although some twenty-five years later, with the engraved frontispiece for *As You Like It* from the 1709 Rowe edition [Fig 32], where
the clothes, the setting and the general atmosphere of this pastoral scene are not
dissimilar. This very early pastoral scene is a surprising production for England in
1709 and one could be forgiven, were it not so firmly dated, for supposing it to be
later. Engraved illustrations to editions of plays, notably of Shakespeare, have been
considered by other writers as evidence of contemporary theatre custom and as implied comment and criticism, but their possible importance as influences on later
artists has tended to be overlooked. Study of these plates might add to our knowledge
of the art of the early years of the century.

The sense of the stage is more evident still in another of Laroon's paintings of two
people, a man and a young woman with a basket of fruit, in a landscape, *The Rencontre*
[Plate 44]†, but the poetry is missing. One of Laroon's duller works it nevertheless adds
weight to the idea that the origin of these scenes is the theatre. The writer of the
entry in the Gallery catalogue suggests that it may be based on a ballad such as
Strawberry Fair – ' "Kind Sir, pray pick of my basket" she said'. No one, after all, was
more likely than Laroon to think of such a subject after spending some of his early
years singing this kind of song in the theatre. The repeated appearance in the fancy
pictures of young women with baskets of fruit and apples may be simply a decorative
cliché, but there is no doubt of the basket's significance in, for example, Act III,
Scene I, of Farquhar's *The Recruiting Officer*, where Plume, a young military man, is
considering the seduction of an innocent market girl:

Plume : Come, I must examine your basket to the bottom, my dear.
Rose : Nay, for that matter, put in your hand; feel sir. I warrant my ware as good as any in
 the market.
Plume : And I'll buy it all, child, were it ten times more.

That the basket as a symbol would be appreciated outside the theatre is suggested by
the publication in 1739 of Faber's engraving after Mercier of this very moment in
the play.[1]

Portraits

Laroon is first mentioned by Vertue as a portrait painter in 1733 when, after com-
menting on his loss in the Charitable Corporation, he refers to 'some portraits in
large from the life. whereby he woud not be uneasy if he coud, (Stoop to it) now to
make some benefit of it. which seems a little aukard to begin with, after 50 four or
five'.[2] Seven years later Vertue remarks that he 'did some portraits from the life well
painted a bold free manner. with good Spirit'.[3] We have only four painted portraits
and a few drawings from which to assess Laroon's ability in this field, but these fully
support Vertue's opinion.

The *Self Portrait* [Fig 33]†, a splendid picture with any amount of panache, was
recently in the London art trade as by an unknown French painter, understandably
as it is in the tradition of the more formal French self-portrait such as the painting
ascribed to Charles-Antoine Coypel in the Musée des Beaux Arts at Tours [Fig 34].
Facing to the spectator's right with the head turned towards the front, the painter is
seated on a chair or stool with a Venetian scroll-back (itself almost a signature),
wearing a puce-coloured cloak. The head is firmly painted but the draperies show
Laroon's characteristic thin translucent paint and sketchy drawing. On a canvas in

front of him are the outlines of a head on a buff ground. Style and technique suggest a date of about 1730, as does the campaign wig which the painter wears. This date is not necessarily contradicted by Vertue whose comments in 1740 may be retrospective and refer to the same portraits which he mentioned in 1733. The missing portrait of 'Mr Swiney' (Owen MacSwiney) which Vertue links with a self portrait cannot have been painted much, if any, earlier than 1730, as it was not until about that year that MacSwiney returned from his long exile in Italy.

Unfortunately there is no certain portrait of Laroon with which to compare it. The head in the Ashmolean *Group of Artists* [Fig 35], probably a little later, is, as far as can be seen, contradictory only in the set of the eyebrows; but it seems that some at least of the identifications in this group are unreliable.[1] A family resemblance to the engraved portrait of his father [Fig 1] may also be noted. The portrait of *James Macardell*, the engraver [Plate 48], was inscribed and dated on the back of the canvas before it was relined: *James Maca/Marcellus Laroon 175(?4)* in Laroon's hand or a convincing copy. The end of the sitter's name was indistinguishable and the final figure of the date uncertain as the canvas edge had perished. Firmly but lightly painted the greyish-brown ground shows through, especially in the face, which, with the hand, holding a porte crayon, is beautifully modelled; and typical of Laroon are the outlining of the features and the highlights on the hand and stock. Macardell's age of twenty-five in 1754 accords with the apparent age of the sitter, whose identity is confirmed by the reasonably close resemblance, allowing for the difference in age, to the self-portrait of 1765, engraved six years later by Richard Earlom.[2] Laroon's portrait illustrates again the difficulty of dating his work for stylistic reasons as I should certainly have suggested, were it not for the inscription, that it had been painted some ten years earlier.

Similar in style is the portrait of a *Gentleman in Brown* [Plate 47]†. Facially not unlike Macardell the young man is informally posed against a background of very sketchy trees. There is no attempt at a realistic setting and the painting can be seen perhaps as depicting a character from a play in front of a backcloth rather than as a true portrait. The fourth portrait [Plate 9]† is of a young man painted on a buff ground; his coat, outlined in green remains the colour of the ground. The face is more solidly painted than in the last two mentioned, a good deal of red being used, and the typical highlights appear. It is unfinished and consequently difficult to date but certainly nearer to the time of the *Self Portrait*; indeed it is the kind of portrait which Laroon shows himself painting.

Of the eleven 'chiefly pencil sketches of very remarkable characters, taken about the year 1725, amongst which are two sketches of Mr Rolus, engraver of the broad seal to King George I' which were sold at the Strawberry Hill sale, one sheet only, the sketches of John Rollos,[3] the seal engraver, can be identified with certainty [Fig 53]. The two heads are different however both in style and in feature and in spite of the authority of the sale catalogue I am inclined to question whether they are of the same person and by the same hand. The lower head is very spirited with a light flickering pencil line of true rococo character and embodies all Laroon's distinction as a draughtsman. The upper head is more linear and less vivid. Sufficiently like Laroon's own portrait of himself it is so much in the format of a drawing for a medal or coin that I suggest that it may be a sketch of Laroon by Rollos. Another drawing which may be one of the Strawberry Hill group is the three-quarter length portrait of a young man reading a book in the collection of Mr Leonard Duke [Plate 7].

Fig 34 Charles-Antoine Coypel?
Portrait d'un artiste
Oil on canvas 36¾ × 28¾ inches
Musée des Beaux Arts, Tours

Fig 35 Artist unknown Head of Laroon (detail from *A Group of Artists*)
Oil on canvas
Ashmolean Museum, Oxford
†Cat Nos 23, 12

1 See M. I. Webb quoted in note 5, p53.
2 Macardell was born in Dublin about 1729, not 1710 as often stated. He was a pupil of John Brooks. About the year of this portrait he established himself at the Golden Head in Covent Garden. He was one of the most skilful and successful mezzotint engravers, until his early death in 1765.
3 According to Vertue, Rollos was Engraver of Seals to the King and Engraver of Stamps to the Stamp Office. He died, aged about sixty, on 16th May, 1743, and was buried at Paddington. He was a fellow member with Laroon of the Rose and Crown Club, where he was known as Ovidius Naso (*Vertue VI*, p33). He may have been identical with the 'Mr. Rollos' who, according to Steele (*The Theatre*, no. 11, 6th February, 1720), invented ' – – – an engine for Hoop-petticoats, which makes them more easy and commodious to the wearer, closes about the limbs in going into a coach – – – , and expands itself when at liberty'.

Cat No 42

Inscribed with initials *C. F.* and an illegible name and dated 1724, it has not been possible so far to identify the sitter.

Two early drawings of men's heads [Figs 59, 60], already mentioned, are generically related to etchings by Lauron, but two later heads of *A Frenchman* and *A German* [Plate 61] appear to be sketches from nature. And there is the interesting early drawing [Fig 61] which, as I have already suggested, is probably a portrait sketch of Lauron by his son.

Conversation Pieces

The *Musical Assembly* [Plate 3] is Laroon's earliest known painting and the one that most nearly fulfils the requirements of the true conversation piece. It is neither signed nor dated and its provenance is unknown until 1819. Dress, wigs and hair-style, and setting, all proclaim that it belongs to the early years of the century, a number of significant details suggesting about 1720 as a likely date. The men's full-bottomed wigs are not exaggeratedly high, and the locks of one, worn by the very modish young man standing in front of the table, hang behind; his coat shows signs of fashionable shortening; the women's dresses are elaborately flounced and the sleeves widen towards the elbow. In addition the cravats of the men and the caps and handkerchiefs of the women are all in keeping with this date. The assembly is taking place in a late seventeenth-century room and the rounded end and turned legs of the harpsichord are those of an early eighteenth-century instrument, very similar to one made by Thomas Hitchcock in about 1720, now in the Victoria and Albert Museum.

If this is a true conversation piece, and not a fanciful assembly, then most if not all of the figures must be portraits; but here we are up against the difficulty of identifying, by comparison, small figures in a group portrait, which is even greater than of equating two lifesize portraits of a sitter by different painters. Without some outside evidence one can only conjecture, but I think it is possible to make suggestions which are neither wild nor improbable. I believe the Knight of the Garter to be Charles Mordaunt, third Earl of Peterborough, who, in 1722, married Anastasia Robinson, the opera singer. Comparison with known portraits of Peterborough shows some resemblance in general appearance.[1] It is true that this man looks younger than sixty-two – his age in 1720 – but from contemporary accounts he appears to have kept his youth very well. Horace Walpole writes that he was 'of an advantageous figure' but even literary portraits can disagree for Swift's description of him, at the age of sixty, is 'a skeleton in outward figure' but with 'more spirits than any young fellow I know in England'. More striking, however, is the closer resemblance of the second figure from the right to Vertue's engraving of Murray's portrait of William Croft, organist of Westminster Abbey and composer of Church music, who was Anastasia's teacher. Her father, a portrait painter, returned from Venice in 1713 after losing his sight, and it may be that there is an oblique reference to this in the group on the right where an old woman is pointing to her eyes in a possibly significant way. Thomas Robinson rented a house in Golden Square, previously owned by Henry Saint-John, Viscount Bolingbroke, where he 'had concerts, and also conversations on certain days in every week, which were the resort of all who had any pretensions to politeness'. This house might be the setting for the scene, although the rural view through the window and the placing of the staircase make it unlikely; or, if the date is after 1722, which I think improbable, it could be Peterborough's house at Parson's Green where Anastasia held musical parties after her secret marriage. But Laroon's

1 Dahl's portrait of 1706 and the engraving after Kneller's portrait of 1705.

architecturally inadequate interiors usually have an element of the fanciful, perhaps of the stage, in them. It would, of course, be satisfactory to point to Anastasia herself but the pose of the woman most likely to be her, next to the Garter, makes identification difficult. There is, however, nothing obviously contradictory between this young woman and the engraving by Grignion of Vanderbanck's portrait. It is, I suppose inevitable that the hunchbacked violinist should be called Pope (only apparently within the present century), but Pope did know Peterborough and Anastasia, corresponded with the Earl and visited his house at Bevis Mount.

Although some of the background figures may well be types, most of the people here, whoever they may be, look too individualised to be other than portraits. The same may be said of only a few of the figures in the other conversations – the *Dinner Party* [Plate 5], the *Nobleman's Levée* [Frontispiece] and the *Musical Tea Party* [Plate 30]. It is the first of these which helps to explain the difficulties both in identifying people and setting, and in establishing the dates of these pictures. Although the related drawing [Plate 4], which is signed, dated and inscribed: *M. Laroon fecit 1719. Presented to King George 1st – a picture I painted in 1725*, is in general composition similar to the painting there are many differences in figures and setting. It will immediately be noticed that the dimensions of the archway with figures of Atlantis supporting the entablature are different; that, in the drawing, the space above the arch is occupied by a large painting of a Commedia dell' Arte scene with Pulcinella and Harlequin; and that the other paintings on the walls are different. The most noticeable change in the figures is in those before the table, where three women in the drawing are replaced by a woman, a man, almost identical with the 'cellist in the *Musical Assembly*, and a page. A glance is enough to see that the faces in the painting bear no resemblance to the conventional representation in the drawing. The only conclusion seems to be that, in 1725, Laroon pulled out from his portfolio this drawing of 1719, and used it as the basis for a painting, improving it as a composition and inserting, among a number of Laroon types, some portraits. Comparison of the second figure from the right in the *Dinner Party* with the second from the left in the *Levée* is convincing evidence of the use of types, but it is difficult to regard all the figures as such, especially in the *Levée*, where the nobleman himself, the stout man on the left the man in profile next to him and several others are firmly individuals.

In composition the *Dinner Party* is related to certain paintings of biblical and religious festivities, such as Veronese's *Marriage at Cana* in the Prado and Jan Steen's *Twelfth Night* at Detroit, rather than to the festive portrait groups of Regents in seventeenth-century Holland where the painter takes care to ensure that every face can be clearly seen whatever the disposition of the figures in these always commissioned works. The resemblance to Veronese's group, the Veronese-like colouring in some of Laroon's paintings, the similarity between the serving-man on the right of the *Dinner Party* and the serving-man on the left of Tintoretto's *Belshazzar's Feast*,[1] and the repeated appearance of Venetian scroll-back chairs and stools, all support E. K. Waterhouse's comment that Laroon's 'un-English' paintings owe something to his stay in Venice.[2] As I have already suggested a second visit to that city, during one of the gaps in his army service, seems to be a probability.

It is interesting also to compare the *Dinner Party* with Detroy's *Le Dejeuner d'huitres* at Chantilly, painted some ten years later, where all the figures are in motion – some needlessly – because they are treated as part of the decorative pattern of which the elaborate architectural setting, with its many caprices, is only another part.

Cat Nos 1, 13
Cat No 4

Cat No 40

1 Vienna Gemäldegalerie.

2 E. K. Waterhouse, *Painting in Britain 1530–1790*, p133.

1 N. Pevsner, *The Englishness of English Art*, 1964, passim and figs. 4a & 4b.

Cat No 3

Cat No 4

2 R. Edwards, 'The Conversation Pictures of Marcellus Laroon', *Apollo*, October, 1935, p196.

3 R. Steele, *The Spectator*, 28th July 1711, no. 129.

4 Notably nos. 1, 19, 25 and 28 in the volume of drawings in the Victoria and Albert Museum entitled *The Exact Dress of the Head, Drawn from the Life at Court, Opera, Theatre, Park etc. By Bernard Lens, in the Years 1725 & 1726 from the Quality & Gentry of ye British Nation*, and also in fig. 33 in A. P. Oppé, *English Drawings at Windsor Castle*, 1950, which reproduces three of the head dresses from a similar volume at Windsor Castle.

5 R. Edwards, 'Conversation Pictures of Marcellus Laroon', *Apollo*, October 1935, p196.

6 O. Millar, *Southill*, 1951, p46 and *Tudor, Stuart and Early Georgian Pictures in the Collection of Her Majesty the Queen*, 1963, p174.
7 I am grateful to Mr Oliver Millar for discussing this picture with me and for considering and convincingly disagreeing with my tentative suggestion that it might represent James Stuart, the Old Pretender, with his two sons.

Laroon's painting reminds us of Pevsner's view that two of the 'polarities' of British art are the vertical and the curvilinear, often to meet but seldom to fuse. When Pevsner wants to demonstrate Hogarth's 'undulating curve' he uses as illustration the figure of the husband from Scene II of *Marriage à la Mode* and not the whole picture.[1] Many of Laroon's individual figures could be used for the same purpose but seldom the whole composition except perhaps the *Village Wedding* [Plate 19].

The early date for the *Dinner Party* has been disputed. Ralph Edwards regards it and the *Levée* as having been painted about the same time as the signed and dated *Musical Tea Party* of 1740 [Plate 30], and suggests even of the *Levée* that it is 'tempting (and not impossible on style and costume) to move the date a few years forward'.[2] I think it is more consistent with costume and style to move the date backwards and to bring it nearer to 1725 than 1740. Indeed the more we see of Laroon's work the more likely it seems that the *Musical Tea Party*, while probably painted in 1740, was based on earlier drawings. Dating by costume is especially difficult in the early eighteenth-century. Fashion moved slowly, and provincial fashion more slowly than in London – a time-lag which is entertainingly described by Richard Steele in *The Spectator* in 1711 '– – – during our progress through the most western parts of the kingdom, we fancied ourselves in King Charles the Second's reign, the people having made very little variations in their dress since that time'.[3] With fashionable assemblies, and these early conversations of Laroon's are nothing if not that, this particular difficulty hardly arises. Some invaluable evidence for these exact years 1725-27 in London is provided by drawings of women's hair-styles and head-dresses by Bernard Lens III.[4] Identical with those in the *Dinner Party* they support, even confirm, this earlier dating, and the probable earlier origin of the *Musical Tea Party*.

The nobleman in the *Levée* has been variously identified as John, Duke of Marlborough, the Duke of Buckingham, Frederick, Prince of Wales and more recently as John, Duke of Montagu. Some military significance can perhaps be read into the great battle-piece on the left-hand wall – quite unlike wall paintings in other works by Laroon – but, even allowing for his practice of using earlier drawings when painting conversations, it seems unlikely that the nobleman could be Marlborough who, born in 1650, became paralysed in 1716 and died in 1722. The Buckingham identification can be demolished on chronology alone[5] and I can see no reason to consider Prince Frederick as a likely competitor. Although I am not convinced of Laroon's association with the Montagu family (see p80) the possible resemblance between the nobleman and portraits of Montagu at Boughton and Hinchingbroke (see Cat. No. 13) and the similarity between the decorative canvases in this picture and the work of the French painters employed by the first Duke of Montagu at Montagu House cannot be discounted.[6] But as with Laroon's other conversations we remain essentially in ignorance.[7]

It is equally difficult to make convincing suggestions about the chamber, its walls hung with a variety of decorative pictures, in which the *Levée* is taking place. Authenticity of setting did not trouble painters of conversations with clearly identifiable figures. Hogarth, for instance, placed the *Wedding of Stephen Beckingham* in a church interior resembling an elaborated St Martin's-in-the-Fields whereas the ceremony is known to have taken place in St Benet's, Paul's Wharf. But Hogarth's setting was recognisable if neither accurate nor authentic. Laroon's settings are never recognisable: the most careful examination has failed to identify even one. His architectural details are unconvincing, mouldings and capitals being often quite improbable. The nearest equivalent to certain features in Laroon's settings is to be found in Marco Ricci's stage designs, the archway with figures of Atlantis in the *Dinner Party* being very similar to an archway in one of Ricci's drawings, while details in the *Levée* recall others.[1] These drawings were not brought to this country until much later in the century, when they entered the Royal Collection from Consul Smith's collection in Venice; but there seems good reason why Laroon, closely connected with the theatre as he was, should have known Ricci's work and probably Ricci himself during his second visit in 1720. The impression left however is not so much of 'influence' as of a similar approach, scenic rather than architectural, to interior detail. Nevertheless the artistic world in the eighteenth-century London was a small one: small enough for painters to know what their colleagues were doing: and borrowing, imitating and copying were not regarded as particularly culpable unless financial rights were infringed. Even Hogarth's objections to piracy of his prints, culminating in the Act of 1735, did not seem to be paralleled by objections to other painters copying his pictures. Garrick can be relied on to be near the truth when he wrote in the prologue to *The Clandestine Marriage*:

> Poets and painters, who from Nature draw
> Their best and richest stores, have made this law:
> That each should neighbourly assist his brother,
> And steal with decency from one another.

It has been suggested that the *Musical Tea Party* [Plate 30], called by Law[2] *A Royal Assembly at Kew Palace* with 'Augusta of Saxe-Gotha, the wife of Frederick, Prince of Wales, and her friends', is, like other Laroon conversations, connected with the wedding in 1730 of the fourth Earl of Cardigan and Lady Mary Montagu. The inscribed date of 1740 is, as we have seen, no argument against this possibility. It is true that the lady pouring out tea is a good deal more like contemporary portraits of the Countess than she is like Princess Augusta, and the equestrian portrait, suggested by a painting such as Van Dyck's *Charles I*, could be the first Duke of Marlborough, the Countess's grandfather. But once again we are in the realms of conjecture. That it is a wedding or betrothal scene is perhaps supported by the small statue of Cupid with bow drawn at the chief protagonists, unless Laroon is here implying a less reputable association.

In two examples, the *Musical Conversations I and II* [Plates 53, 54] a late dating for stylistic reasons – the emphatic outline, the wash-like paint and the brush-point highlights – is supported by costume and especially wig style. In both paintings most of the men wear a small wig tight to the head with a queue or bag, belonging to the middle years of the century. In the *Musical Conversation II* the second standing figure from the left wears the type of campaign or travelling wig which was going out of fashion in the same years. And the short 'buckled' wig of the sixties, worn by the cleric beside the door, recalls the rather later one described by Samuel Foote in 1774, in *The Cozeners* – 'I am sure you must admire his dear wig; not with the bushy, brown buckles, dangling and dropping like a Newfoundland spaniel; but short, rounded off at the ear, to shew his plump cherry cheeks; white as a curd, feather-topped, and the curls as close as a cauliflower'.[3]

These assemblies of less individualised people take place in a less aristocratic milieu – in smaller, lower rooms with modest furniture and with pictures on the walls, chiefly landscapes and seascapes, of a type which Laroon did not paint himself and

1 See A. Blunt and E. Croft-Murray, *Venetian Drawings at Windsor Castle*, pp41–5 and plates 70 and 76.

2 E. Law, *Kensington Palace . . .*, 1899, no. 54.

Cat No 4

Cat Nos 27, 28

3 Quoted by C. W. and P. Cunnington, *English Costume in the Eighteenth Century*, 1957, p245.

1 Coll. Mr & Mrs Paul Mellon.

2 Walpole Society, *Vertue III*, p65.

3 *Ibid.* p100.

4 A. Blunt and E. Croft-Murray, *Venetian Drawings at Windsor Castle*, reproduce Joseph Goupy's caricature of Heidegger as fig. 29, p165, and an engraving from it as fig. 27

Cat Nos 48, 49

Cat No 84

which do not appear to reproduce the work of any specific painter. Unlike Hogarth, Laroon nowhere uses pictures for symbolic purposes, although the statuary, as in the *Tea Party*, may occasionally serve this purpose. With the exception of the *Musical Assembly* it is probably correct to regard the conversations as largely fancy pictures – in which some figures may be portraits and some architectural details may be real. The very successful composition, in particular the integration of the separate groups of figures, reinforces this view. They may be compared for instance with Gawen Hamilton's previously mentioned *Club of Artists* or with Charles Philip's *Tea Party at Lord Harrington's House*.[1] In these there is a stiffness of grouping and a lack of cohesion extremely difficult to avoid when a number of people, whose faces must all be seen and must all be 'like', are painted, with due regard for social precedence, in their authentic setting.

Of outstanding interest because they are unique in English art – and as far as I know in the art of any other country at this time – are the *Music Party* drawings [Figs 54, 55 Plates 10, 18, 22, 23, 24]. Finished drawings intended as works of art in their own right, and preliminary sketches, they are doubtless referred to by Vertue in 1773 '– – – he lately has amusd himself more particularly to painting & drawing. conversations. in small with much variety & pleasant entertainment of musick'[2] and again in 1740 'Some large drawings of merry makeings – etc. on a sheet of paper black lead & washt. in Frames & Glases – well drawn & good Spiritt & design – of these he made presents – some to Friends & Gentlemen of his acquaintance'.[3] I know four finished drawings, the sketches for two of these, a sketch and a larger pencil drawing of the same subject, and a sketch for an engraving of a music party. The finished drawings are in pen over pencil, some with wash, and measure between $13\frac{1}{2}$ and 18 inches in height and between $10\frac{1}{4}$ and $13\frac{1}{4}$ inches in width. The sketches in pencil are smaller. Inscriptions on two, *made a finished Drawing of this for Mr Carbonelli 1731* and *The finishd Drawing for Mr Bendall Martyn: Secretary to the Excise: 1733* confirm Vertue's comment.

The identification of the people in Laroon's conversations, drawn or painted, has been bedevilled by Horace Walpole's inscription on the *Music Party* drawing [Plate 24] now in the British Museum that 'the gentleman on the left under the door is John, 2nd Duke of Montagu; the lady standing by him is his 2nd daughter, Mary Countess of Cardigan, afterwards Duchess of Montagu'. With or without reason it seems that nearly all the conversations have, at some time or other, been given the Montagu label. Walpole's inscription cannot have been written before 1766, thirty years after the date of the drawing, because it was not until this year that the Dukedom was conferred on the Earl of Cardigan; nor is the figure referred to by Walpole very like other portraits of Montagu, and the same figure in the sketch bears no resemblance at all. Other rather tenuous reasons for associating Laroon with the Montagu family are his acquaintance, during his army days, with the Duke of Marlborough, the Countess's grandfather; the appearance at the harpsichord, in this drawing, of John James Heidegger 'the ugliest man in London' who was known to the Montagu circle;[4] and the possible association of the *Musical Tea Party* with the wedding of Lady Mary Montagu.

Two groups of men sitting and standing round a table, inscribed *Designed for Mr Mat. Ashton* and dated *1732/3* [Plates 11, 12], not with music as the theme, are equally lively pencil sketches of merrymakings. Another pencil drawing, inscribed *Father & five Sons. eldest artist. 2 in ye Army two at Sea* [Plate 14], unquestionably a portrait group and so like the sketches for Mat Ashton that it can confidently be dated to just this time, may be the sketch for the painting mentioned by Vertue in 1733 as 'a very large family peice valud at several hundred pounds'.[1]

The *Officer and Lady at Supper* [Plate 26], a small painting on the borders of conversation and 'fancy', shows a young man in blue with a young woman in Laroon's characteristic puce-pink and a serving man in red. The heavier colours on the right are effectively balanced by a red cloak thrown over the back of the woman's chair. Our attention is drawn to the glasses which seem to have been painted very consciously as a piece of virtuosity. The same may be said of still-life objects in other paintings, notably the magnificent wine fountain in the *Dinner Party* and the 'cello leaning against a stool in the *Musical Assembly*. The *Officer and Lady at Supper* is closely related to another painting and two drawings which must, in spite of their decorum, be brothel scenes. The *Interior with figures* [Plate 45] has, besides the four young people, an older woman to whom attention is drawn by her rather extravagant gesture. It is not perhaps until one looks at the drawing of a *Conversation* [Plate 42], where the old woman is dressed in the traditional bawd's costume and the exchange of erotic glances between the couple is explicit, that one realises the significance of this figure.

1 Walpole Society, *Vertue III*, p64.

Cat No 16

Cat No 22

Cat No 95

Caricature and Genre
If 'the true end of satire is the amendment of vices by correction', Laroon cannot be regarded as a satirist. He observed his fellow men with amusement and used caricature often so slightly as to bring to mind the narrow distinction between 'character' and 'caricature'.[2] That he occasionally expressed some criticism may be admitted but comparison of the *Frenchman at Bow Street* [Plate 30] or *Night Walkers brought before a justice of the peace* [Fig 36],† with Hogarth's *Woman swearing a child to a grave citizen* [Fig 37] shows Laroon's citicism, even if there at all, to be vague and undirected. This is true except of those paintings and drawings which include the figures of beggars, from the *Riders and Beggars* of 1735 [Plate 21]† to the late drawing *Charity* of 1772 [Plate 67]†. As social comment with an element of criticism these imply that

†Cat Nos 93, 52, 64

2 Hogarth intended his engraving of *Characters and Caricatures* to demonstrate the difference between the two categories, and Fielding expands the argument in the preface to Joseph Andrews. The twentieth-century eye would however tend to see caricature in some of Hogarth's 'characters'. For the engraving and the relevant quotations see R. Paulson, *Hogarth's Graphic Works*, 1965, vol. I, pp188–9 & vol. II, pl. 174.

Fig 36 Marcellus Laroon *Nightwalkers brought before a justice of the peace*
Pencil, pen and brown ink 7¾ × 9¾ inches
Sabin Galleries, London (Cat No 93)

Fig 37 William Hogarth *Woman swearing a child to a grave citizen* Oil on canvas 19½ × 26 inches
National Gallery of Ireland, Dublin

1 R. H. Wilenski, *Dutch Painting*, 1945 edition, p35, ' – – – the Emperor's tour of 1549 – – – while a musician performed upon an organ. The sounds emitted from this organ were of an unusual character, for a cat with its tail tied to a key was imprisoned in each pipe and as the musician struck the notes the tails were pinched and the cats screeched and howled'. The source of this quotation is not stated.

Laroon was at least aware of injustice if he had none of Hogarth's moral force; and overt awareness was rare enough in the first half of the eighteenth century. His compassion did not extend to animals and the *Execrable Concert* [Fig 49], derived apparently from a Netherlandish tradition where 'music' is produced by pulling the tails of cats imprisoned in a box,[1] emphasizes the immense difference between the attitudes of Laroon and Hogarth, whose engravings of *Four Stages of Cruelty* had been published some twenty years earlier.

Fig 39 William Hogarth
The Sleeping Congregation
Oil on canvas 21 × 17½ inches
Minneapolis Institute of Arts

Fig 38 Marcellus Laroon *Alms-men* pencil 11¼ × 14⅜ inches
National Gallery of Scotland, Edinburgh

Cat No 41

Cat No 76

But in a quiet, undemonstrative way Laroon is making fun of people – what is his *Alms-men* of 1720 [Fig 38] but a less forceful *Sleeping Congregation* [Fig 39] which Hogarth painted eight years later? Perhaps Hogarth had seen the drawing, but I mention the likeness only at once to point out the difference between Laroon's slightly caricatured scene, quite free from didacticism, with its bored congregation in a small intimate church and Hogarth's painted sermon with a sleeping one in a baroque edifice. Laroon has been referred to as 'an imitator' of Hogarth but it is abundantly clear that his social comment and caricature, whether they form the main theme or are merely an intrusion into a fancy picture, derive from his father's work and from the Dutch-Flemish low-life tradition.

One early caricature group *Grotesque Musicians* [Plate 1] is indeed so like Lauron's work as to have been attributed to him but, apart from general stylistic resemblances to the son's work, the central figure of the young violinist is unmistakably Laroon's. Of particular interest as his earliest caricature – I should date it to the first few years of the century – the violinist and the player of the one-stringed fiddle anticipate similar figures in the *Execrable Concert* of some seventy years later.

Two personal caricatures, *Laroon and Reisen* [Fig 63] and *Mat Ashton at Chester* [Plate 6] have lost point because the circumstances are unknown, and the comments of Ashton's friends have been erased. Except for these and one or two others, notably the *Farmer apprenticing his son* [Plate 13] and *An Ancient Couple* [Plate 17], where the two old people have rather animal-like faces, Laroon's use of caricature is very limited. An element of jest can be seen in a number of the conversations pieces, only one or two figures being picked out, except in the *Levée* where the nobleman himself and several other figures are subtly, even slyly, caricatured. Nevertheless I find it impossible to agree with Antal who, mentioning the *Levée* specifically, saw Laroon as an ancestor of Thomas Patch.[1] Patch was caricaturing the visitor to Rome, the noble connoisseur and the modish conversation piece – Laroon an occasional individual in an otherwise straight drawing or painting. Patch's ancestor was Pier Leoni Ghezzi and Ghezzi may have had a marginal influence on Laroon. There is a compositional resemblance between the *Frenchman at Bow Street* and Ghezzi's drawing of *Philip von Stosch and Roman Antiquaries*,[2] but I fail to see any real relationship between individual figures by these two artists, the resemblances being probably fortuitous.

The three surviving drawings of scenes of military life are the *Execution of Deserters* and *Market Tent in Camp* [Figs 15, 16] both of 1707, and *Broken on the Wheel* [Plate 2]. The *Market Tent* is a convivial scene reminiscent of Dutch low-life pictures, but in which Laroon 'types' appear, the young 'cellist and the two figures on the extreme right, and a recurring motif, seen so often in Dutch seventeenth-century paintings, the pouring of wine from a bottle held high above the glass. Many of Laroon's characteristics can be seen in this early drawing: his difficulty in effectively articulating joints; the thin spidery fingers; the use of the cross formula for placing the features; the occasional ambiguity in action rather than movement; and the very successful figure of the 'cellist, drawn with vigour and correctness as only a practising musician could.

The *Execution of Deserters*, seems, like the *Market Tent*, to be a spontaneous sketch of an actual event; but the two figures on the right rather give the impression that they may have been added later. It and *Broken on the Wheel* – an exceptionally fine drawing of a most revolting subject realistically treated – show a somewhat unexpected side of Laroon's nature, a callousness, even a brutality, which carries no undertones of protest. Perhaps it is unfair to judge from only two drawings as the implied horror in Callot's *Les Misères de la Guerre* is not apparent so much in the individual plates as in the cumulative effect of the whole series. Laroon's *Execution* recalls to some extent Callot's plate of *L'Arquebusade* but more reminiscent of Callot is the 1771 drawing of *Charity* [Fig 40] in its resemblance to the hospital plate [Fig 41] in *Les Petites Misères*. Laroon may well have owned one or both sets of Callot's prints as his collection of 'Prints, Books of Prints and Drawings' was important enough to warrant a sale of its own, separate from the sale of paintings.

It was in the *Village Wedding*, as I have already mentioned, that Laroon successfully united the two conflicting strands of his art. In contrast the drawing of the *Wedding Night* [Plate 32] is realistic, with close Dutch affinities and with more than a touch of caricature. It is the only graphic representation that I have seen of throwing the stocking, a traditional custom when continuing the marriage festivities in the bridal chamber. Here Laroon in his acute observation of human appearance and in giving

Cat No 79

Cat No 80

Cat Nos 46, 83

1 F. Antal, *Hogarth*, 1962, p243, n. 30.

2 Albertina, Vienna. Reproduced in L. Lewis, *Connoisseurs and Secret Agents in Eighteenth Century Rome*, 1961, pl. 4.

Cat Nos 38, 37, 77

Cat No 64

Cat No 94

Fig 40 Marcellus Laroon *Charity* Pen and brown ink over pencil with wash $16 \times 24\frac{1}{2}$ inches
Ashmolean Museum, Oxford

Fig 41 Jacques Callot *Les petites misères de la guerre* Engraving by Callot

Cat No 46

1 F. Antal, *Hogarth*, 1962, p184.

what seems an inevitably true report of human behaviour comes closest to Hogarth, just as in the earlier *Farmer apprenticing his son* [Plate 13] he seems to anticipate Rowlandson.

The complex evolution of the English equivalent of the Dutch low-life scene from Egbert van Heemskerck, Lauron and their contemporaries, through Hogarth to the social caricatures of Rowlandson who, as Antal so aptly said 'continued the spirit of the rococo, albeit in a grotesque Dutch vein', [1] owes something to Laroon.

In comparing Hogarth and Laroon, the writer of the introduction to the catalogue of the 1964-5 British Museum exhibition of Hogarth's drawings and engravings so rightly remarks that Laroon's 'figures are more stilted but there is the same close observation of the setting whether for high or low life and the same attempt to make his point by gesture and expression' but I find myself hardly agreeing with his further comment that 'like Hogarth he observed human nature with a detached eye to expose it.' In those drawings, the *Wedding Night* [Plate 32] and the *Frenchman at Bow Street* [Plate 31]†, where Laroon closely approaches Hogarth in his observation of human frailties and follies, there is little true satire, little criticism of behaviour. While apparently drawn from nature some of his most vivid characters are remarkably like figures in his father's work [Figs 42, 43] and one should, I think, be careful not to accept too readily that all his figures were directly observed, even in such a drawing as this. His figures are often more stylised, less individualised; and it is interesting to compare the decorous French-influenced scenes, which I have suggested are of brothels [Plates 42, 46]† where the right true end seems in doubt, with one of his father's vigorous and forthright Dutch mezzotints [Fig 13] where the end is inevitable and soon.

Laroon's powers of observation were not comparable with those of Hogarth, who could capture the significant attitude, movement or gesture with a few lines. He does occasionally approach very close with certain subjects, notably with figures of musicians. If Laroon's 'cellist in the *Market Tent* [Fig 44] be compared with the rather similar figure in Hogarth's drawing of *A Card Party* [Fig 45] my point will be made. Laroon's man is playing his instrument, Hogarth's is merely holding his with the bow resting on the strings. Laroon, as a practising musician and a 'cello player himself, knew the feel of the bow on the strings and knew the pressure of the fingers on the fingerboard – Hogarth did not.

Two paintings, which have already been used to demonstrate the change in Laroon's style, the *Tavern Interior* of 1742 [Plate 35]† and the *Card Players* of 1760 [Plate 52]†, especially the latter, are so reminiscent of Teniers as almost to amount to pastiche. Certain figures, the old woman aloft, the woman with her back towards us and the two quarrelling men look as if they might be direct borrowings but I have not been able to find the originals; and from what we know of Laroon's earlier work direct borrowing was not one of his habits. The *Tavern Interior* is still quite rococo in style, as one might expect from its date, and Antal's words about Rowlandson might well be applied to this painting.

Fig 44 Marcellus Laroon
Detail of 'cellist from Figure 16

Fig 45 William Hogarth *A Card Party* (detail)
Pencil, pen and brown ink and grey wash G. D. Lockett

† Cat Nos 94, 56, 95, 5, 9

Fig 42 Marcellus Laroon
Wedding Night (detail) Drawing
British Museum

Fig 43 Marcellus Lauron
Scene in a Tavern
Etching

Late Drawings

Seventeen drawings, mostly genre scenes with some figure studies, belong to the last few years of Laroon's life. The earliest inscribed date is 1770 but Reitlinger records one of 1768 in the series which includes *The Quarrel*, *The Duel* and *Wounded* [Plates 63, 64, 65]. It is unfortunately missing but there is no reason to doubt that 1768 is correct for these works. Other drawings are dated *1772*, the year in which the artist died. Many of the upright examples are of a size much favoured by Laroon, about 19 by 13 inches but the horizontal ones are twice this size, roughly 18 or 19 by 27 or 28 inches. Drawn with a reed pen and usually in brown ink over very light pencil, some of these big vigorous drawings are quite remarkable productions for a man in his tenth decade. The broken staccato line, equivalent to the brushpoint highlights of some of the late paintings, gives a sense of movement, even of restlessness, which is stabilised by the ruled lines of the background buildings. Laroon presumably adopted this technical trick of the broken line to disguise the tremor of his ageing hand, and used a ruler only where the straight unbroken line was essential.

As a crowd scene the most successful is *Cudgeling* [Plate 66] with the clever handling of more than a hundred figures, many surprisingly well characterized, and with little repetition except for the man on the extreme right who appears, with slight variations, in four other drawings. Most satisfactory as a composition is *Charity* [Plate 67] perhaps because it appears to be based, in reverse, on the hospital scene in Callot's *Les Petites Misères de la Guerre*. Equally vivid and amusing are *A High Wind* [Plate 71], and *The Fight* [Plate 68], where town waits and citizens are fighting with swords and musical instruments while the watch looks helplessly on. Some of the smaller upright drawings, *Cavalrymen on the march* [Plate 72] and *Street Scene* [Plate 74] for instance, are just as lively.

The genesis of these late drawings is difficult to establish. In some the underlying pencil is much firmer and suggests that they may have been unfinished sketches lying in his portfolios which he worked up many years later, but there is no difficulty in accepting the pen work and the slightly tremulous signatures and inscriptions as belonging to the last part of the artist's life; or in accepting the whole group as evidence of continuing artistic vitality in one of great age.

They are, in addition, of considerable interest as social record because they seem to be drawings of observed events, either contemporary or from the painter's long memory. *Cudgeling* is, as far as I know, the only graphic representation of a sport which was widespread but apparently especially practised in the west country. In 1715 Dudley Ryder notes that:

'Mr. Samson told us of a very odd sort of a custom in the West of England. Cudgelling it seems is a mighty diversion among them and it's handed down from father to son. The father teaches his sons to cudgel by playing with them himself and never allows them to spare him, but when they have once broke his head he then thinks them fit to shift for themselves and go into the world. There was a father cudgelling with his son and the young man was afraid to strike his father who continually pressed him to it. "Sirrah", says he, "why dont you strike me?" But the boy refused until the father at length gave him a smart blow that raised his spirits and the young rogue had courage enough to break his father's head. "That is well done" says the father. "Now you are fit to go into the world." It seems they beat one another most furiously, and the father will set his children to cudgel and stand by and encourage them to thrash one another.'[1]

It is not, I think, stretching the evidence too far to see the influence of theatrical illustration in some of these splendid drawings, especially in *The Fight* [Fig 46] where

Cat No 65

Cat No 64

Cat No 70

Cat No 103

Cat Nos 68, 72

1 Dudley Ryder, *The Diary of – – –* . 1715–16, transcribed and edited by W. Matthews, 1939, p35. For this sport see also J. Eyles, *Backsword or Singlestick?*, Country Life 8th July, 1965, p108.

the background buildings can be paralleled very closely in an engraving for *The Humorous Lieutenant* in the 1711 edition of Beaumont and Fletcher's plays [Fig 47]. But *The Fight* also appears to be a record of almost journalistic immediacy although no melée of this kind is, to my knowledge, referred to in diaries or in the contemporary press.

Fig 46 Marcellus Laroon *The Fight* Pen and brown ink over pencil with wash $17\frac{3}{4} \times 27\frac{1}{4}$ inches
Ashmolean Museum, Oxford

Fig 47 Francois Boitard
The Humorous Lieutenant
Engraving

Epilogue

Fig 48 Cornelis Troost *Performance of 'Het Verliefde Bregje' in a garden* Oil on canvas $30\frac{1}{2} \times 46$ inches
Private Collection, Netherlands

1 The twelve 'Pamela' paintings were bought for the Nation and were then divided between the Tate Gallery, the Fitzwilliam Museum and the National Gallery of Victoria, Melbourne. They were brought together again for the Highmore exhibition at the Iveagh Bequest, Kenwood, in 1963, four being reproduced in the catalogue.
2 F. Antal, 'Mr Oldham and his Guests by Highmore', *Burlington Magazine*, vol. XCI, 1949, pp128–32.
3 L. Gowing, 'Hogarth, Hayman, and the Vauxhall Decorations', *Burlington Magazine*, vol. XCV, 1953, pp4–19.

Until fairly recently Hogarth has occupied a lofty and somewhat lonely eminence as the only British artist of the first half of the eighteenth-century deserving serious consideration in the history of art. During the last few years painters have started to emerge from what might be called the Hogarth background. Joseph Highmore, for instance, after his *Pamela* series had been included in the sale room catalogues in 1920 as by Cornelis Troost,[1] and his portrait group of *Mr Oldham and his Guests* had entered the collection of the Tate Gallery in 1948 as by an unknown painter (rescued by the percipient eye of Frederick Antal[2]), can now be seen as a considerable artist. Francis Hayman, whose important collaboration with Hogarth at Vauxhall has been explored by Lawrence Gowing,[3] is revealed as a prescient and very lively painter. Both still await their monographs, as, to mention only three, do John Wootton, Samuel Scott and Philip Mercier, on all of whom work is in progress. Many others, not perhaps deserving such extended study, are still figures of varying remoteness, whose works are attributed, largely by chance and tradition: Bartholomew Dandridge, Charles Philips, William Hoare, the Heinses of Norfolk and other expatriate foreigners, Peter Angillis, Pierre Parrocel, Joseph van Aken, Joseph Nollekens the elder and so on. Indeed the list could be extended several-fold.

The position with some of the latter group is much the same as with Laroon in 1907 when, as I have already noted, Randall Davies knew only two paintings and three or four drawings. Laroon's tally today is thirty-five paintings and sixty-seven drawings, and they continue to emerge. I am well aware that this catalogue of Laroon's work is necessarily incomplete. More of his paintings must remain to be discovered, relegated still perhaps to the attics of private houses or to the basements of galleries and museums, and it is inconceivable that there are not more, perhaps many more, drawings awaiting the light of day; but enough can now be seen to form an opinion of his ability, of his relationship to other painters and of his contribution to the formative years of the British school of painting.

Berenson suggested that the only reasons for studying minor masters were the fun of the chase and the winnowing of the oeuvre of the great; both legitimate enough reasons, the former highly enjoyable and the latter of unquestioned value. There seems however to be this added reason, at least for eighteenth-century England, that only by studying the minor masters can a perspective view of the artistic scene be obtained: of its intricate social, literary and theatrical associations, and of its ties with European art, some aspects of which Antal has defined in his exhaustive study of Hogarth.

Repeatedly in discussing Laroon's work I have compared or contrasted it with Hogarth's, an unfair juxtaposition because of Hogarth's originality of conception, his astonishing powers of observation and of characterisation, and his natural gift for applying paint. But if Laroon was a little master beside Hogarth he was not so little compared with his nearest European equivalents, Pietro Longhi in Venice, and Cornelis Troost in Amsterdam [Fig 48]. Troost, of Dutch birth and training but working under similar French influences, was consistently more competent (although I know of no painting by him to outweigh the *Village Wedding*), more versatile both in his media and genre and far more prolific, as befitted a highly professional painter. His approach however was identical: humorous but only slightly satirical, his observation modified by literature and the theatre, his poetry mixed with the mundane, and his intimate stage scenes, conversation pieces and portraits, comparable with Laroon's work, always more successful than his large formal portraits and portrait groups.

The complex Dutch-French influences on English art in the eighteenth century have yet to be fully charted but they are seen with some clarity in Laroon's paintings.[1] In his versatility, his subject matter, his immediate response to the world around him and to musical and theatrical associations and in his receptive but selective attitude to European art, Laroon embodies many of the characteristics of painting in England in the first half of the eighteenth-century; while his sense of poetry and his delightful feeling for colour, his humorous observation and his never-failing vitality contribute to his artistic personality.

1 For instance the shadowy association of Troost with English print-makers needs elucidation. A print in mezzotint of a *Corps de Garde* scene (after a pastel drawing in the collection of the Koninglijk Oudheidkundig Genootschap in the Rijksprentenkabinet at Amsterdam) was made by 'C. Corbut' (R. Purcell) for Robert Sayer. And there is a photograph in the Rijksbureau at the Hague, of a version of Troost's *Wedding of Kloris and Roosje* which is said to be signed *J. Faber* and dated, but unfortunately the date is not recorded.

Fig 49 Marcellus Laroon (after) *The Walpole-Scott Club*
tracing by John Thomas Smith $10\frac{11}{16} \times 14\frac{7}{8}$ inches
Mrs G. F. H. Bligh

THE LAROON FAMILY

Marcellus (Marcel) Lauron

Laroon writes, according to Smith's transcript, that 'My father's as well as grandfather's name was spelt Marcellus Lauron; – – – My grandfather, Marcellus Lauron, was a native of France, by profession a Painter, and lived in Holland many years. It never came to my knowledge where he married, or of what country his wife was. At the Hague he had several children'. Buckeridge states that the grandfather came to England bringing his son 'being very young' with him. As mentioned in the text it was thought until recently that, despite Laroon's statement, the family name might have been spelt *Laurens* on the evidence of two drawings tentatively attributed to the grandfather: one a sketch from an etching by Place after Barlow signed and dated *M aurens fec AEt 75½ 1696*. (Collection Lord Methuen) the other a commemorative design of the founding of the Bank of England, signed *MLaurens inv. fecit AEt 74* (Collection the Bank of England). It now seems likely that this draughtsman was Mark Laurens or Laurence of St Martin, Outwich, described in the Bank's records as accountant, who had accounts in Bank Stock, who died on 25th February, 1705/6 and who from his will can be seen to have no connection with the Lauron family.

In the following notes as in the text Lauron refers to the father and Laroon to the son, Captain Marcellus Laroon.

Jan I – elder brother of Lauron

Laroon writes that 'My father's elder brother, as well as my father, was a Painter, and remained in Holland and died there; his performances were not greatly esteemed'. Jan married Francina Jans, daughter of Jan Willems, and was involved in two law suits in 1674 and 1684, neither concerned with painting, but Jacob Matham, presumably the painter, being also involved (from the archive notes of Dr Bredius, kindly communicated by Dr S. J. Gudlaugsson).

No works by Jan I are known.

David

Mentioned in Wurzbach and in Bénézit as 'Maître dans la gilde de la Haye en 1732'. He was perhaps a son of Jan I.

No works by him are known.

The family of Marcellus Lauron

Besides John and Marcellus Laroon the children born to Elizabeth Lauron (née Keene) were:

Elizabeth, christened October 1682, died young.

James, christened March 1683/4, living in 1701.

Elizabeth, christened March 1688/9, living in 1701.

Charles, christened August 1690, probably died young as he is not mentioned in his father's will in 1701.

These entries are in the registers of St Paul's, Covent Garden (*Publications of the Harleian Society, Registers*, vol. XXXIII, 1906 pp62–81). The registers at Chiswick, where the marriage may be presumed to have taken place and where John and Marcellus III were probably christened, do not begin until 1678, nor has the entry relating to Marcellus, who was born, according to his own statement, in 1679, been found elsewhere.

Elizabeth, the wife, appears to have died before 1701, the date of her husband's will, in which she is not mentioned. No record of her death or burial has been found, nor has any information about James or the daughter Elizabeth come to light. What little is known about John will be found in the text.

Appendix II

REMBRANDT IN YORKSHIRE

The arguments for a visit to this country by Rembrandt are based on a statement by Vertue and the existence of some drawings by Rembrandt of English scenes.

Vertue's statement in notebook 21, 1 1 1, p6 (Walpole Society, *Vertue I*, p29) reads:

'Renbrant van Rhine was in England livd at Hull in Yorkshire about sixteen or eighteen months where he painted several Gentlemen & sea faring mens pictures. one of them is in the posession of Mr. Dahl, a sea captain with the Gentlemans name. Renbrants name & York & the year 1662/1. Christian.'

and alongside 'reported by old Larroon who in his youth knew Renbrant at York'. The word 'Christian' implies that Lauron's account was handed on by this informant, who is likely to have been Charles Christian Reisen. In the transcript in notebook 23068 p3 (*Vertue I*, p29, notes 6 and 7) the identical wording is used but above 'Gentlemens name' is 'no' and after 'York' is 'not so'. These additions appear to be in Vertue's hand and if they are accepted the chief piece of evidence, 'York' in the inscription on the portrait, is lost.

There are four drawings by Rembrandt of scenes in England, *St Alban's Cathedral*, *Windsor Castle* and two similar views of *London with Old St Paul's*. One is dated 1640, one doubtfully 1640 and two are undated. Many differing opinions have been expressed about them, Otto Benesch (*The Drawings of Rembrandt*, 1955, vol. IV. p210) stating categorically that 'None of the English views was drawn from nature or can be brought forward as a proof that Rembrandt visited England'. That they were drawn from engravings or other drawings is likely as the perspective in the St Alban's and in both London scenes is tentative and incorrect, and imaginary features, such as the monumental steps in the St Alban's are introduced. Even if they are accepted as views from nature it is generally agreed that they could not be as late as 1661.

No evidence of any kind to support Vertue's statement has been found in Hull or York.

The more important articles on the problem are:

H. de Groot, 'Heeft Rembrandt in Engeland vertoefd', *Oud Holland*, 1897, pp193–8.

A. M. Hind and A. E. Henderson, 'Rembrandt's Supposed Drawing of Old St Paul's, *Burlington Magazine*, 1910, vol. XVII, pp334–40.

H. de Groot, 'Rembrandts reizen naar Engeland', *Oud Holland*, 1921, pp1–10.

G. Wimmer, 'Das Problem der Reise Rembrandts nach England', *Die Graphischen Kunste*, 1936, pp144–52.

C. White, 'Did Rembrandt ever visit England?', *Apollo*, May 1962, pp177–184.
It is a fascinating question, but however much as a true Yorkshireman I should
like to think of Rembrandt in my native town of Hull, I do not believe that any of the
very insubstantial evidence for a visit is acceptable. After all even Vertue may have
nodded occasionally.

Fig 49a Marcellus Laroon   *The Execrable Concert*
Pen and brown ink over pencil with wash $7\frac{1}{4} \times 9\frac{1}{4}$ inches
Mr & Mrs Paul Mellon

THE CRYES OF THE CITY OF LONDON

Description

The Cryes of the City of London, a small folio volume, contains up to seventy-four plates, depending on the edition. The page size, untrimmed, is approximately fifteen by nine inches, and the dimensions within the plate mark vary between nine and ten, and between six and seven inches. There is a first and a second title, identical in lettering:

The Cryes of the City of London Drawne after the Life.

Les Cris de la Ville de Londres Designez apres La Nature.

L'Arti Comuni che vanno per Londra Fatte dal Naturale.

P. Tempest excudit Cum Privilegio.

with below the base line of the engraving *M.auron delin: P. Tempest exc:* Each title has a different engraved figure, the first a man and the second a woman.

After the plates were passed to H. Overton, about 1709–11, identical additions were made to the titles except that the second title has no date. The first title now reads:

The Cryes of the City of London Drawne after the Life. In 74 Copper Plates

Les Cris de la Ville de Londres Designez apres La Nature.

L'Arti Comuni che vanno Londra Fatte dal Naturale.

P. Tempest excudit. cum Privilegio

with below the base line *M.auron delin: Printed & Sold by Henry Overton at the White Horse without Newgate, London 17 (?) 11 P. Tempest exc:*

Plate numbers were added in the right lower corner.

Editions and Impressions

All recorded editions or impressions known to the writer are listed, and those of which copies have been examined are clearly differentiated.

A *Term Catalogue* announcements.

1687, Michaelmas term. (Arber, II, p207)
'The Crys of *London*, both Men and Women, drawn after the Life, in variety of Actions and Habits: curiously engraven upon Copper-plates, fit for the Ingenious and lovers of Art, . . . sold by P. Tempest, over against *Somerset* House, in the *Strand*.'

1687/8, Hilary term. (Arber, II, p218).
'The Crys of *London*, newly drawn after the Life, both Men and Women, in variety of Actions and Habits; curiously Engraven upon forty Copper-Plates, fit for the Ingenuous (sic) and Lovers of Art . . . Sold by P. Tempest, over against *Somerset* House, in the *Strand*.'

1688, Trinity term, (Arber, II, p231)
'The Crys and Habits of *London*, both Men and Women, drawn after the Life, in great variety of Actions and Dresses; curiously Engraven upon sixty Copper-plates; being fit for the Ingenious and Lovers of Art. Printed and Sold by P. Tempest over against *Somerset* House, in the *Strand*.' (C. L. Hindley in *A History of the Cries of London*, 1881, p90, however quotes correctly the *London Gazette* for May 28th–31st, 1688, i.e. Trinity term, as giving "Curiously Engraven upon 50 Copper Plates").

No copies of any of these editions have been found, but in support of there having been an edition with sixty plates is the fact that the number of plates of the dismembered copy in the Pepysian Library is exactly sixty and that they are exceptionally clean, fresh and therefore early impressions.

Arber (I, pXI) points out that not all the books listed in the *Term Catalogues* were actually published at that time, and that the description was often inserted from what we should call a proof title-page, in advance of publication. It seems very improbable that four separate and differing announcements would be made before publication but there is a real possibility that volumes corresponding to some of these descriptions were not published. Not too much should be read into the failure to locate copies of these early editions as only one copy is known of the Michaelmas 1688 edition (see below). Books of this kind are ripe for cannibalising which could account for the disappearance of any number of copies. I have seen many separate plates, but nearly all are numbered, which identifies them as coming from the 1711 edition.

B

1688, Michaelmas term. (Arber, II, p240)
'There is now compleatly finished, The Cryes and Habits of *London*, newly drawn after the Life, in great Variety of Actions and Dresses; curiously Engraven upon Seventy-two Copper-plates, fit for the Ingenious and all Lovers of Art, Sold by P. Tempest, over against *Somerset* House, in the *Strand*.'

The only one known copy is in the London Guildhall Library. It has two plates inserted, *Any Bakeing Pears* and *New River Water*, presumably by a previous owner to 'complete' it, as it was described when sold at Hodgson's, 25th October, 1946, as '72 engraved plates . . . should be 74'.

1689, Trinity term. (Arber, II, p281).
'There is now compleatly finished, The Crys and Habits of London, both Men and Women; newly drawn after the Life, in great variety of Actions and Dresses; curiously engraven on 74 Copper-plates, fit for all lovers of Art . . .'

One certain copy (British Museum) and one probable copy (County Hall Library, Westminster) of this edition are known. The British Museum one is firmly identified by its seventy-four plates and by the date *1692* on the title which accompanies the cipher of a previous owner, Narcissus Luttrell. The order of the plates is different from all others but there is little doubt that it was disturbed when re-bound.

D   1709, 1711, 1731, 1733

1709, Easter and Trinity Term. (Arber, III, p647).
'The Cries and Habits of the City of *London*, drawn after the Life. By Mr Laroon. Engraven on Copper; and printed on 74 sheets of paper . . . printed for, and sold by, P. Tempest at the Golden Head in *James Street, Covent Garden;* and at the Italian Coffee House in *Katherine Street*, in the *Strand*.'

No certain copy of this edition is known, and the only rather marginal support for its existence is that copies of the *Cryes* were available in 1710, Z. C. van Uffenbach, *Oxford in 1710*, 1934, p164–5, remarking, on 27th October, that ' . . . we went to a print dealers and bought the 'Cryes of London' in seventy-four sheets for half-a-guinea. In these engravings all those persons who hawk cheap wares, crying them in the streets, are represented from life with the words that they cry. They are similar to the 'Cris de Paris' '. Van Uffenbach also mentions an edition 'with notes, for the curious tones that they call or sing can be freakishly imitated on the violin', which is quite unknown.

1711, *The Postman*, 6th to 8th February, according to MS. note on the Guildhall copy (Guildhall II).
'The Cries of the City of London, consisting of 74 Copper-plates, each Figure drawn after the Life, by the famous M. Laron. Etched and engraved by the best Workmen, each plate is printed on a half sheet of demy paper, price 10s a set. Sold by H. Overton at the White Horse without Newgate, by Overton at the Golden Buck near St Dunstans church in Fleet Street.'

No copy unequivocally dated *1711* is known, but a number have a date on the first title which can be variously read as *1711, 1731*, or *1733*. These all have added to the first title 'In 74 Copper plates', and to both titles 'Printed and Sold by Henry Overton at the White Horse without Newgate, London'. The engraving of the date is crude and the two final italic numerals in all copies examined are not clear and could well be read *31* or *33*.

After this edition, whatever its true date, the *Cryes* cease to be mainly of Lauron interest as, in the next edition of about 1750, published by Robert Sayer, and in subsequent editions, many of the plates were re-engraved with alterations after L. P. Boitard, and ten plates were replaced by eight new ones.

Two plates, numbers 24 and 71, which bear the name of the engraver J. Savage, are enough to establish his style, his weak drawing and his predilection for cross-hatching. A number of unsigned plates can be attributed to Savage, but it is possible to see the work of other engravers in many plates, especially numbers 8, 16, 41, 65, 73, and 74.

It has often been supposed that Tempest himself was responsible for some, or even many, of the plates, but *excudit* should be read to mean no more than published. No engraving incontrovertibly by Tempest is known, nor does his name appear in Vertue's lists of engravers. Vertue also has a nice comment on the use of *excudit* – '2 prints lately done after Teniers And publisht by B. Baron. he cunningly put excudit but they are sd to be done by some young man he employs now not his own hand . . .'.

List of Plates

The order given is that of the 1711 edition. In this the plates are numbered whereas in the earlier editions they are not and the order consequently varies a good deal.

1 (First title)
2 A Sow Gelder
3 Any Card matches or Savealls
4 Pretty Maids Pretty Pinns Pretty Women
5 Ripe Strawberryes
6 A Bed Matt or a Door Matt
7 Buy a fine Table Basket
8 Ha Ha Ha Poor Jack
9 Buy my Dish of great Eeles
10 Buy a fine singing Bird
11 Buy any Wax or Wafers
12 Fine Writeing Inke
13 A Merry new Song
14 Old Shooes for some Broomes
15 Hott Bak'd Wardens Hott
16 Small Coale
17 Maids any Cunny Skinns
18 Buy a Rabbet a Rabbet
19 Buy a Fork or a Fire Shovel
20 Chimney Sweep
21 Crab Crab any Crab
22 Oh Rare Shoe
23 The merry Milk Maid
24 The merry Fidler
25 Lilly white Vinegar 3 pence a quart
26 Buy my Dutch Biskets
27 Ripe Speragas
28 Maids buy a Mapp
29 Buy my fat Chickens
30 Buy my Flounders
31 Old Cloaks Suits or Coats

32 Fair Lemons & Oranges
33 Old Chaires to mend
34 Twelve Pence a Peck Oysters
35 Troope every one one
36 Old Satten Old Taffety or Velvet
37 (Second title)
38 Buy a new Almanack
39 Buy my fine singing Glasses
40 Any Kitchin Stuffe have you maids
41 Knives Combs or Inkhornes
42 Four for Six pence Mackrell
43 Any work for John Cooper
44 4 Paire for a Shilling Holland Socks
45 Colly Molly Puffe
46 Six pence a pound fair Cherryes
47 Knives or Cisers to Grinde
48 Long Thread Laces Long & Strong
49 Remember the Poor Prisoners
50 The Squire of Alsatia
51 London Curtezan
52 Madam Creswell
53 Merry Andrew
54 A Brass Pott or an Iron Pott to mend
55 Buy my 4 Ropes of Hard Onyons
56 London Gazette here
57 Buy a White Line, a Jack Line, or a Cloathes Line
58 Any Old Iron take money for
59 Delicate cowcumbers to pickle
60 Any Bakeing Peares
61 New River Water
62 The Spanish Don
63 Merry Andrew on the Stage
64 The famous Dutch Woman
65 Mountabanck
66 The famous Dutch Woman
67 Josephus Clericus Posture Masterius
68 Clark the English Posture Master
69 The London Begger
70 John the Quaker
71 The London Quaker
72 Oliver C: Porter
73 A Noncomformist Minister
74 Frater Mendicans

The titles of the plates are in English, French and Italian, except 53 and 71 which are in English only and 67 and 74 which are in Latin only.

Each plate has *M.Lauron* or *M.auron, del* or *delin* and *P.Tempest, ex, exc* or *excud, Cum Privilegio*. Plate 24 has, in addition, *J. Savage Sculptr. A:O: et S:R:* and plate 71, *J. Savage Sculp*.

Description

The Art of Defence is a small folio volume with twenty-four plates and a frontispiece. The page size is approximately nine by fourteen inches and the dimensions within the plate-mark vary between seven and eight and three-quarters, and between eleven and a half and twelve and five-eighths inches. Lauron's name does not appear on the plates of the three known copies. The attribution depends on Vertue's statement that Lauron's 'most considerable works. besides paintings are designs he made for a book of ye London Cryes another for fencing . . .', on the similarity in style and technique of the drawing for plate 8 (Fig 12) to the drawings for the Cryes (Figs 7, 8) and to the small initialled drawings on cards (Fig 11) and on there being no other plates of fencing of the approximate date which bear any resemblance to Lauron's work.

Impressions

The Art of Defence is a bibliographical puzzle. The *Term Catalogue* for 1699 records two impressions, one in Trinity term (Arber, III, p141):

'The Art of Defence; in which the several sorts of Guards, Passes, Encloses, and Disarms, etc are represented in 50 proper Figures: with their respective Explications. Price, stitcht, 1s. 6d. . . . sold by Phillip Lea at the Atlas and Hercules in Cheapside.'

and one in Michaelmas term, under 'Reprinted' (Arber, III, p163):

'The Art of Defence; in which the several sorts of Guards, Passes, Enclosers, and Disarms, etc are represented by proper Figures: with their respective Explications. The only Original Book of Fencing. Price 3s. 6d.'

Bibliotheca Annua for 1699 p54 records one impression:

'The Art of Defence, in which the several sorts of Guards, Passes, Enclosures and Disarms, etc. are represented by their proper Figures, with their respective Explications, etc. p. 3s.6d. Printed for J. Marshall in Gracechurch-street.'

Known copies

Only three copies have been traced, two in the British Museum and one in the Pepysian Library. Of the Museum copies one is in the Department of Prints and Drawings and one, bound in at the back of H. Blackwell, *The English Fencing-Master* (1705), in the Library (C.135.d.1.). They are identical, except for the order of the plates, both having the frontispiece with title '*The Art of Defence In which several sorts of Guards, Passes, Encloses, and Disarmes etc are represented by proper Figures with their respective Explications. W Elder sculp: Sold by G Beckett at ye golden head in the old Baily.*' There are twenty-four plates, besides the frontispiece, of which twenty have engraved titles and four plates 12, 17, 18, and 19 have hand-written titles. The copy in the Pepysian Library has been dismembered and the plates mounted in one of Pepys's two large volumes *My Collection of Prints & Drawings relating to London & Westminster etc – Put together Anno Domini 1700* (Pepys MS 2973). The frontispiece with title is missing and the plates have been wrongly titled in manuscript *The London Fencing Master Publisht by George Narville Turner, ye Moor, Native of London Schollar to the sometime La Croix & Himself a celebrated Master of Defence, in the said City, for more than 30 years; as he still is this present Anno Domini. 1700.* No book entitled *The London Fencing Master* appears to be recorded nor is anything known of George Narville Turner. It may be that he is represented by the turbanned figure in the Lauron plates. Of the plates in the Pepysian copy, 17, 18 and 19 have engraved titles. The engraved titles on 9 and 12 appear to have been cut off and 9 has a pencilled title on the subject.

Plates

Frontispiece. The Art of Defence In which the several sorts of Guards, Passes, Encloses, and Disarmes etc, are represented by proper Figures with their respective Explications.

1 A Pary with the left hand
2 A Cart in Tierce over the Arme
3 Tierce in Cart in the Cart Side
4 A Thrust in the Flanconade
5 Here a Teirce is cutt off by a Cart by turning about the left foot (with the Body) in makeing the Pass
6 A very good Secure upon the Shell with the Point ready to be offered
7 Here is the French Guard (the Knees being bent but very litle) and the Guard and Posture does prevent a pass on ye outside of ye Sword, so that whichsoever of the two shall make a Pass, he must give it in Second, or by a disengage in Cart. etc.
8 The Sword and Dagger Guard: The Sword that offers first is Defended by ye Dagger
9 A forc'd Thrust in Cart
10 A Pary and Thrust in Tierce
11 A Teirce cutt off (in time) by a Second.
12 with Advancing the Left foot the Sword of the offending party is put by and the Deffendant makes his point Good for teirce.
13 A Cart Guard
14 A Disarme in Cart
15 A Thrust in Cart
16 The Pass here given is a Teirce, which on the inneside of the Defendants Sword ought to have been made in Cart, but that the Dagger of the Offendant does secure it in this Figure.
17 Another Guard In Cart
18 Spanish Rapier And Dagger
19 A fflanconade uppon the turne
20 A Disarme in Cart
21 Here is a Secure upon the Shell with the point offered
22 A Disarme in Tierce
23 A Disarme in Second
24 A Parry and Disarme in Tierce

The names of the engravers appear on some plates only: *W. Elder* on the frontispiece and plates 6, 8, 14 and 23, and *S. Moore* on plate 4.

Appendix IV

LETTER FROM LAROON III TO HIS BROTHER JOHN

Translated from English and published by J. C. Weyerman in
De Leevens-Beschryvingen der Nederlandsche Konst-Schilders, 1729–69,
vol. IV, 2nd pagination 32–3.

Geliefde Broeder!

   *Thans ben ik werkelyk geoccupeert in het toebereiden van myn Patroontas, en
verdere Oorlogs-gereedschappen, ten einde om morgen door de dop te worden
geschooten in het bestormen van de Fransche en Beijersche Linien. Ik denk aldaar een
Vaandel te winnen, of in het gras te byten, want in myn tegenwoordig beroep van een
vrywillig doodslager, schat ik een eerlykedood hooger als een eerloos leeven. De Dood
is zo verschrikkelyk niet als de Menschen wel praten, want de Dood is het einde van
alle vreeze, en het begin der gelukzaligheit, en geen Man sterft zo vrywillig, als die
eerlyk wandelt op deeze akelige baan des vergankelyken Leevens. De Dood, Broer
Jan, is de schaar die den draad van 's Menschen zorg afknipt, doch eerloosheit is het
beginzel aller zorgen.*

   *Maar, Broeder Jan, dewyl ik weet, dat je zo een groot Theologant niet zyt als den
Bischop van Cangor, zal ik uw zeggen, dat men de Dood verdeelt in drie artykels,
gelyk als onze Regiments-exercitie. De eerste Dood is de scheiding tusschen de Ziel en
het Lighaam, benevens de Lighaams-ontbinding tot den Dag des laatsten Oordeels.
De tweede is de Dood der Zonde, dewyl die Man word als dood gegroet, die te
rusten legt in de zonde. En de laatste is de Eeuwige Dood, tot dewelke de
Goddeloozen zullen worden veroordeelt ten laatsten dage.*

   *Zo veel Godgeleerdheit heb ik reeds overgegaart in het gezelschap van des
Generaals Kapellaan; en indien ik 'er een Kompagnie by overgaren kan voor het
einde van den Veldtogt, zal ik in allen deelen vergenoegt zyn van myn eerste
Kampagne.*

   *Vaar wel, Jan Broer, ik cryg vaak, en daar van zal ik my thans bedienen, want
met het krieken van den Dageraat zal de Artillery, Keteltrom, de mindere
Tymbaalen, de Trommels, de Trompetten, et het Dood-muzik van het grof en klein
Handgeschut, de vaak wel uit de oogen houden van uw Broeder,*

Den Volontair, N. Laroon.

Schellenberg,
's Nachts voor de Bataille, in
July 1704.

Bibliography

CONTEMPORARY SOURCES – MANUSCRIPT AND PRINTED

Avery, E. L. *The London Stage 1*, pt. 2 (Carbondale, Illinois, 1960)

Avery, E. L. and Scouten, A. H. 'Tentative Calendar of Daily Theatrical
Performances in London (1700–1701 to 1704–1705)', *Proceedings of the Modern
Language Association*, LXIII (1948), 114–180.

Buckeridge, B. *An Essay Towards an English School of Painters*, appended to
R. de Piles, *The Art of Painting* (3rd edition 1750).

Dalton, C. *English Army Lists and Commission Registers, 1661–1714* (1892–1904).
... *George the first's Army 1714–1727* (1910–12).

Graham, R. *A Short Account of the most Eminent Painters*, appended to Du Fresnoy,
The Art of Painting, first edition 1695, second, with additions 1716.

Hake, H. M. 'Some contemporary records relating to Francis Place ...',
Walpole Society X (1921–22) 39–69. British Museum, Stowe MSS 746.

Harleian Society Publications–Registers XXXIII (1906) *The Registers of St. Paul's
Church, Covent Garden, London*.

Knowles, J. A. 'Henry Gyles, the Glass Painter of York', *Walpole Society* XI
(1922–23) 47–72. British Museum, Stowe MSS 746.

Smith, J. T. *Nollekens and His Times* (1828, edited by W. Whitten 1920).

Vertue, G. *Notebooks*. Walpole Society XVIII, XXII, XXIV, XXVI, XXX
1929–30 to 1948–50, Notebooks, I, III, IV, V, VI.

Walpole, H. *Anecdotes of Painting* (1762–71).

Westminster Library, Ratebooks of St. Paul's, Covent Garden.

Weyerman, J. C. *De Leevens-Beschryvingen der Nederlandsche Konst-schilders ...*
(The Hague and Dordrecht 1729–1769).

Croft-Murray, E. and Hulton, P. *The British Museum, Drawings by British Artists, Volume One: XVI & XVII Centuries* (1960).

Borenius, T. 'The Kaleidoscope of Taste', *The Studio*, December 1931, 351–365.
... 'Marcellus Laroon and John Wooton', *Country Life*, 4th May 1935, 94–98.

Davies, R. *English Society of the Eighteenth Century in Contemporary Art* (1907)
...*Chats on Old English Drawings* (1923).

Edwards, R. 'The Conversation Pictures of Marcellus Laroon (1679–1772)', *Apollo*, October 1935, 193–198.
... 'Conversation Pieces at Kensington Palace by Marcellus Laroon', *Country Life*, 27th November 1937, 94.
...*Early Conversation Pictures* (1954).

Granger, James (continued to 1727 by Mark Noble) *Biographical History* (1806).

Millar, O. *Southill: A Regency House* (1951).
... *The Tudor, Stuart and Early Georgian Pictures in the Collection of her Majesty the Queen* (1963).

Oppé, A. P. *English Drawings, Stuart and Georgian Periods, at Windsor Castle* (1950).

Raines, R. 'Marcellus Laroon the Younger I', *The Connoisseur*, December 1957, 241–245.
... 'Marcellus Laroon the Younger II', *The Connoisseur Year Book 1959*, 113–122.
... 'Marcellus Laroon the Younger and the Commedia dell' Arte', *The Art Quarterly* (Detroit) Summer 1962, 108–112.
... 'Drawings by Marcellus Lauron – "Old Laroon" – in the Pepysian Library', *Apollo*, October 1965.

Reitlinger, H. *Old Master Drawings* (1922).

Sitwell, S. *Conversation Pieces* (1936).

Waterhouse, E. K. *Painting in Britain 1530–1790* (1953).

Whitley, W. T. *Artists and their Friends in England 1700–1799* (1928).

Wilenski, R. H. *English Painting* (1943)

Williams, I. A. *Early English Watercolours*... (1952).

GENERAL WORKS (which are referred to in the text or are among those consulted).

Adhémar, J. *Watteau* (Paris 1950).

Antal, F. *Hogarth and his place in European Art* (1962).

Avery, E. L., Scouten, A. H. and Van Lennep, W. *The London Stage I, II, III* (1960–65).

Bardwell, T. *Practice of Painting* (1756).

Beckett, R. B. *Hogarth* (1949).

Berkeley, G. *Works of George Berkeley* 9 volumes (1948–57) Vol. VIII. Letters of ––– ed. A. A. Luce. (1956)

Blunt, A. *Art and Architecture in France 1500 to 1700* (1953).

Blunt, A. and Croft-Murray, E. *Venetian Drawings at Windsor Castle* (1957).

Bridge, F. *The Old Cryes of London* (1921).

British Museum, Department of Manuscripts, Add. MS. 34788, J. Thornhill, Diary of a journey from London . . . to Holland from 21 May to 19 June 1711.

. . . Add. MS. 39167, A Folio Tract called the Virtuosi or St. Luke's Club.

Burney, C. *A General History of Music* (1776–89).

Churchill, W. S. *Marlborough, his Life and Times* (1933–8).

Cibber, Colley. *Apology for the Life of Mr. Colley Cibber* (1740).

Cole, C. *Memoirs of Affairs of State . . . 1697 to 1708* (1733).

Collins Baker, C. H. 'Antonio Verrio and Thornhill's early Portraiture'. *Connoisseur*, pp10–13 (1953).

Croft-Murray, E. *Decorative Painting in England* (1962).

Cunnington, C. W. and P. *English Costume in the Eighteenth Century* (1957).

Dacier, E. and Vuaflart, A. *Jean de Jullienne et les Graveurs de Watteau au XVIIIe siècle* (Paris 1922–29).

Deane, J. M. *Journal of the Campaign in Flanders. 1708* (1846).

Downes, J. *Roscius Anglicanus* (1708, 1886 edition).

Flower, N. *Handel* (1923).

Gentleman's Magazine

'Green, John' (Townsend, G. H.) *Evans Music and Supper Rooms, Covent Garden, Odds and Ends about Covent Garden* (n.d, ca. 1850).

Grove, G. *Dictionary of Music and Musicians* (1880 edition).

Gudlaugsson, S. J. *De Komedianten bij Jan Steen en zijn tijdgenooten* (The Hague 1945).

Hawkins, J. *History of Music* (1776, 1963 edition).

Hindley, C. L. *A History of the Cries of London* (1881).

Hogarth, W. *The Analysis of Beauty* (1753, ed J. Burke 1950).

Kane, R. *Campaigns of King William and Queen Anne* (1745).

Limojon de Saint Didier *La Ville et la République de Venise* (Paris 1680).

Manchester, Duke of *Court and Society from Elizabeth to Anne* (1864).

Millar, O. and Whinney, M. *English Art 1625–1714* (The Oxford History of English Art, VIII, 1957).

Merchant, W. M. *Shakespeare and the Artist* (1959).

Misson, M. *A New Voyage to Italy* (English translation, second edition 1699).

Odell, G. C. D. *Shakespeare from Betterton to Irving* (1921).

Oppé, A. P. *The Drawings of William Hogarth* (1948).

Paulson, R. *Hogarth's Graphic Works* (1965).

Pevsner, N. *Academies of Art, Past and Present* (Cambridge 1940). ... *The Englishness of English Art* (1956).

Pye, J. *Patronage of British Art* (1845).

Rey, R. *Quelques satellites de Watteau* (1931).

Ryder, Dudley *The Diary of . . . 1715–1716* (ed. W. Matthews 1939).

Smart, A. *The Life and Art of Allan Ramsay* (1952).

Stanhope, P. H. Viscount Mahon *History of the War of Succession in Spain* (1832).

Steegman, J. *The Rule of Taste from George I to George IV* (1936).

Stow, J. ed J. Strype *A Survey of the Cities of London and Westminster* (1720).

Taylor, A. and H. *1715 : the story of the rising* (1936).

Uffenbach, Z. C. van *London in 1710 from the travels of* . . . (translated and edited by W. H. Quarrell and M. Mare 1934).

Walpole, Horace, *Correspondence*, ed W. S. Lewis 1937. Continuing.

Webb, M. I. *Michael Rysbrach, Sculptor* (1954).

Wilson, F. P. 'Illustrations of Social Life III: Street Cries', *Shakespeare Survey*, XIII, (Cambridge 1960), 106–110.

Catalogue of Paintings and Drawings
by Marcellus Laroon

The catalogue is divided into the following five sections devoted to: dated paintings
(1 to 9); undated paintings (10 to 36); dated drawings (37 to 72); undated drawings
(73 to 107); and other recorded works (107 to 120).

In addition to the title, the date or assigned date and details of present ownership
are given in the margins of the pages.

Dimensions are given in inches and centimetres, height first.

DATED PAINTINGS   Cat Nos 1–9

1   A DINNER PARTY
1725   Plate 5

SIZE 36 × 33⅞ in / 91.4 × 86 cm

MEDIUM Oil on canvas.

DATED 1725 (from the associated drawing).

PROVENANCE The inscription on the related drawing (40) implies that this painting was in the collection of George I by 1725. It first appears, however, in the inventories of the Royal Collection in 1818, when it was no. 505 in the MS. catalogue of pictures at Kensington Palace, *An Entertainment containing a Number of Portraits of distinguished persons. M. Laroon;* and subsequently as no. 812 in Law's catalogues of Hampton Court in 1881 and 1898 as *Vanderbank?*; and as no. 53 in his catalogue of Kensington Palace in 1899 as *M. Laroon?*

LITERATURE T. Faulkner, *History and Antiquities of Kensington* (1820), p402; R. Davies, *English Society of the Eighteenth Century in Contemporary Art* (1907), pp34–5; R. Edwards, 'The Conversation Pictures of Marcellus Laroon (1679–1772)', *Apollo*, October 1935, p196; G. B. Hughes, 'The Old English Banquet', *Country Life*, 17th February 1955, p474; O. Millar, *The Tudor, Stuart and Early Georgian Pictures in the Collection of Her Majesty The Queen* (1963), p174.

NOTES In a very handsome chamber nine elegant young people, in various shades of blue, grey, red and puce, are seated round a table, the host, in old gold with the blue riband of the Garter, pouring wine into a glass. A clergyman, a flautist and numerous attendants, in low tones of grey, brown and blue, stand behind the table. A particularly splendid wine fountain, not in the related drawing, ostentatiously occupies the lower left corner. Through a window on the extreme left some ironwork can be seen on which is a crown surmounting possibly a monogram.

The following suggestions have been made for the identity of the nobleman: Frederick, Prince of Wales, (J. Law, *Kensington Palace*); the Duke of Wharton (Faulkner), the Duke of Montagu (R. Davies and O. Millar).

G. B. Hughes, 'The Old English Banquet' *Country Life*, 17th February 1955, p474, suggests that this painting shows a Fruit Banquet and not a Dinner Party.

The relationship with the drawing of 1719 (40), the identities of the people and the dating are discussed on p77.

HM The Queen, Kensington Palace

2 LOVERS IN A GLADE (I)
1731　Fig 19

SIZE 16¾ × 13¼ in / 42.5 × 33.7 cm

MEDIUM Oil on canvas.

SIGNED AND DATED *M. Laroon. 1731.*

PROVENANCE With Roland, Browse and Delbanco, before 1950; Stephen Roper; with Gooden and Fox Ltd; Christie's, 21st June 1957 (86); with R. A. Lee.

Collection unknown

NOTES For discussion of this painting and similar subjects (nos. 25, 29, 61, 113) see p65.

3 THE VILLAGE WEDDING
1735　Plate 19

SIZE 43 × 37½ in / 109.2 × 95.3 cm

MEDIUM Oil on canvas.

SIGNED AND DATED *Marcellus Laroon. F.1735,* (on the tree trunk on the right).

PROVENANCE Sir Osbert Sitwell.

LITERATURE T. Borenius, 'The Kaleidoscope of Taste', *The Studio*, December 1931, p356.

EXHIBITIONS London, Magnasco Society, October–November, 1925 (22), as *Allegorical Scene*; London, Blairman and Sons, *Marcellus Laroon*, 1951 (7).

NOTES A large number of people are shown in procession through and around a rocky defile. It is an evening scene painted in browns and greens with touches of other colours – the girl on the left in pink, the woman riding pillion in blue with pink hair ribbon and the lady riding in blue. The man riding, partly hidden by the tree, is a clergyman.

Private collection, England

4 A MUSICAL TEA PARTY
1740　Plate 30

SIZE 36 × 28 in / 91.4 × 71.1 cm

MEDIUM Oil on canvas.

SIGNED AND DATED *Mar. Laroon. F. 1740.*

PROVENANCE Presented by Humphry Ward. First recorded in Law's catalogue of Kensington Palace, 1899 (54), as *A Royal Assembly in Kew Palace,* and later in his *Kew Palace,* 1924 (23).

4 A MUSICAL TEA PARTY *continued*

LITERATURE R. Davies, *English Society of the Eighteenth Century in Contemporary Art* (1907), pp34–5; O. Millar, *Southill: A Regency House* (1951), p47; O. Millar, *The Tudor, Stuart and Early Georgian Pictures in the Collection of Her Majesty The Queen* (1963), p174.

NOTES The lady seated at the table is in blue, the man leaning on her chair in grey, the lady filling the teapot in orange yellow with red heels, the seated military figure in a red coat with blue cuffs and the standing man on the far left in white. On the right the group round the harpsichord are in black, white, grey and brown and the man and woman sitting on the stool in light brown and puce with red heels. The curtains are greenish-blue and the dog lies on a red cushion.

One of the music books on the floor has an inscription which is illegible except for a few letters, possible *Cos – – / S – – – / Op – – / S – –*.

The following suggestions have been made for the identities of the people: '– – – some Royal Assembly, apparently Augusta of Saxe-Gotha, the wife of Frederick, Prince of Wales, and her friends in Kew Palace. The Princess in blue is pouring out the tea; – – – Handel is at the harpsichord, and "Orator" Henley close by. The equestrian portrait on the wall appears to be George II', (J. Law); 'the Duke and Duchess of Montagu', (R. Davies and O. Millar).

For a fuller description of the difficulties of identifying the figures in Laroon's conversations see pp 76-81.

HM The Queen, Kensington Palace

5 TAVERN INTERIOR WITH PEASANTS
1742   Plate 35

SIZE 18½ × 15¼ in / 47 × 38.7 cm

MEDIUM Oil on canvas.

SIGNED AND DATED *M. Laroon F. 1748.*

PROVENANCE Christie's, 21st July 1933 (76); with H. A. Sutch, 1938; Captain Richard Briscoe.

EXHIBITIONS London, Blairman and Sons, *Marcellus Laroon*, 1951, (not in the catalogue).

Michael Bevan,
Longstowe, Cambridgeshire

NOTES Painted in low tones of brown and greenish-blue on a buff ground.

6 SCENE FROM 'HENRY THE FOURTH, PART I'
1746   Plate 34

SIZE 35½ × 28¼ in / 90.1 × 71.8 cm

MEDIUM Oil on canvas.

6 SCENE FROM 'HENRY THE FOURTH, PART I' *continued*

Mr & Mrs Paul Mellon,
Upperville, Virginia

SIGNED AND DATED *Mar: Laroon. F. 1746.*

PROVENANCE Douglas Eyre of Landford, Wiltshire, 'always in the family'; Giles Eyre.

NOTES Falstaff, on the left, in a grey jerkin with a red coat round his shoulders, and Bardolph in red, are here seen at the moment when Mistress Quickly enters in Act III, Scene III.

See also p69 where it is suggested that Falstaff is a portrait of James Quin.

---

7 THE WOODMAN
1748   Plate 41

Michael Bevan,
Longstowe, Cambridgeshire

SIZE 35½ × 27½ in / 90.1 × 69.9 cm

MEDIUM Oil on canvas.

PROVENANCE Christie's, 12th March 1937 (48), *A Road Scene with a lady and gentleman enquiring the way from a woodcutter*; with H. Davis, 1940; with Leggatt Brothers; Captain Richard Briscoe.

EXHIBITION London, Blairman and Sons, *Marcellus Laroon*, 1951 (5).

NOTES Against a background of low-toned brown and green, except for the sunset sky, red behind the figures and blue above, the woman wears an old gold dress and hat and red shoes, and the man a grey coat and black hat.

This painting is dated 1748 from the associated drawing (60).

---

8 JAMES MACARDELL
175(?4)   Plate 48

Henri-Philippe Crombé,
Brussels

SIZE 23½ × 15¾ in / 59.7 × 40.0 cm

MEDIUM Oil on canvas.

SIGNED AND DATED *Marcellus Laroon 175(?4)* on the back of the canvas.

INSCRIBED *James Maca – – –* on the back of the canvas.

PROVENANCE With the Sabin Galleries, 1962.

NOTES A half-length portrait of a young man facing left. He holds a porte-crayon in his right hand.

The identity of the sitter is confirmed by the reasonably close resemblance, allowing for the difference in age, to the self portrait of 1765 engraved by Richard Earlom in 1771. The signature and inscription can no longer be seen as the painting was relined while in the possession of the Sabin Galleries.

9 THE CARD PLAYERS
1760   Plate 52

Private Collection,
Beirut

SIZE 25 × 21 in / 63.5 × 53.3 cm

MEDIUM Oil on canvas.

INSCRIBED *Marcellus Larroon Invenit & pinxit 1760. Anno Aetatis 80.*

PROVENANCE In York until 1955 in the possession of the descendants of a Mr Bagley of London; Christie's, 1st April 1955, (66); with John Mitchell, 1955.

NOTES The inscription is probably an inaccurate copy of an original signature and inscription rather than an invention, the *Anno Aetatis* ringing true. The date fits stylistically.

UNDATED PAINTINGS   Cat Nos 10–36

10 A MUSICAL ASSEMBLY
1715–20   Plate 3

SIZE 40 × 50 in / 101.6 × 127 cm

MEDIUM Oil on canvas.

PROVENANCE Etched by George Cruikshank in 1819 to illustrate the *Catalogue of a Collection of Pictures, of that Ornament of the British School, William Hogarth* (a copy of this very rare catalogue is in the Sir John Soane Museum, London). The paintings were sold by private contract at 20 Lower Brook Street, by the dealer Thomas Gwennap, whose name does not however appear. This catalogue states 'by a memorandum found among Hogarth's papers after his death' that the picture 'appears to have been painted for Lord Castlemain; of course intended for Wanstead House' but that it remained in Hogarth's possession and was bought at the sale of his effects by an 'ardent admirer' from whom it was acquired much later by Gwennap. The attribution is as unreliable as the key to the print which identifies the principal figures as Lord Castlemaine (wearing the Garter) and Frederick, Prince of Wales, while others are said to be the Princesses Augusta, Amelia and Caroline, the Earl of Bute, Lord and Lady Walpole, Lady Pembroke, Viscount Boyne, Addison and Churchill.

The painting was apparently confused, perhaps intentionally, by Gwennap, with *An Assembly of twenty-five figures for Lord Castlemaine*, ordered from Hogarth in 1729 which, in 1819, was in the possession of the Hon. William Pole Long-Wellesley (R. B. Beckett, *Hogarth* (1949) p46); Christie's, 14th December 1934 (34) from the collection of Mrs Baker of Malvern, as by Hogarth, (a letter in the Witt Library, from Horace Wallich to the Director of the Courtauld Institute in 1934, states that it had been in Mrs Baker's family for a great many years); Sir Herbert Hughes-Stanton; Christie's, 16th June 1939 (21), from the collection of Lady Hughes-Stanton, as by Laroon; HRH The Duke of Kent.

LITERATURE R. Edwards, 'The Conversation Pictures of Marcellus Laroon (1679–1772), *Apollo*, October 1935, pp196–8; S. Sitwell, *Conversation Pieces* (1936) p72; R. Edwards, *Early Conversation Pictures* (1954) pp57, 165.

EXHIBITIONS London, Blairman and Sons, *Marcellus Laroon*, 1951, (1); Liverpool, Walker Art Gallery, *Painting and Sculpture in England 1700–1750*, 1958 (31).

NOTES In a large room an elegant young woman, in a puce dress with blue collar and cuffs, is singing to the accompaniment of harpsichord, played by another woman, two violins, 'cello, oboe and lute. Slightly to the right of centre a Knight of the Garter, also dressed in puce with the blue riband, another woman and a very modish young man in blue stand listening. On the far right a man in brown is talking to a clergyman. Other groups of people, dressed in various shades of blue, brown and cream, as are the musicians, make up a total of twenty-five figures.

The identities of the people are discussed on pp76–7 where it is suggested that the chief personages are Charles Mordaunt, third Earl of Peterborough, Anastasia Robinson, the singer, and William Croft, the musician. In this connection it is interesting and perhaps relevant (but see p64) that in the sale of Peterborough's 'Furniture' on 16th May 1726, there were four 'conversations', one by 'Horseman', one by 'Nolekins' and two by unnamed painters. Horemans and Nollekens both painted small groups not unlike Laroon's.

HRH Princess Marina,
London

11   SELF PORTRAIT
c 1730   Fig 14

SIZE 32 × 26 in / 81.3 × 66 cm

MEDIUM Oil on canvas.

PROVENANCE With the Sabin Galleries, 1962.

NOTES A half-length portrait turned to the right with the head facing the front. The artist, sitting on a chair or stool with an ornamental scrolled back, wears a puce-coloured cloak and holds his palette which is set with only six colours: clockwise from the thumb-hole, light blue, dark greenish-blue, two shades of brown, reddish-brown and vermilion. On a canvas in front of him is the outline of a face with touches of red on a fawnish-brown ground.

This may be the self-portrait referred to by Vertue in 1740 (*Vertue* III, p100) – 'some portraits from the life well painted a bold free manner. with good Spirit. his own picture Mr. Swineys. and others as big as the life.'

The identification of this painting as a self-portrait of Laroon is discussed on pp74–5.

Mr & Mrs Paul Mellon,
Upperville, Virginia

12   A GENTLEMAN IN GREEN
c 1730   Plate 9

SIZE 28 × 24⅝ in / 71.1 × 62.5 cm

MEDIUM Oil on canvas.

PROVENANCE Mrs Cox of Windsor.

Private Collection, England

NOTES A half-length portrait on a fawn ground of a young man turning to the left with his right hand showing from under his cloak which is outlined in green. The face is more solidly painted than the cloak and hand which appear to be unfinished.

13 A NOBLEMAN'S LEVÉE
c 1730   Frontispiece

SIZE 37 × 30 in / 94 × 76.2 cm

MEDIUM Oil on canvas.

PROVENANCE First recorded by Hawkins (see below and p78) who does not state its whereabouts; at Southill Park since before 1815, when it is recorded in the catalogue. It seems just possible that it was lot 88 in the sale of John Tomlinson's paintings 'collected during a period of nearly forty years' at Christie's on 13th June 1806, 'Hogarth The Levy of a Prime Minister, full of character and genuine humour for which this Artist stands unrivalled.

EXHIBITIONS London, Magnasco Society, October 1926 (2); London, 25 Park Lane, *English Conversation Pieces*, 1930 (125); London, Royal Academy, *English Taste in the Eighteenth Century*, 1955–6 (101), as *The Duke of Montagu's Levée*; London, The Iveagh Bequest, Kenwood, *The Conversation Piece in Georgian England*, 1965 (28).

NOTES In a fine baroque chamber, a nobleman, dressed in puce and wearing the blue riband of the Garter, is holding his levée. Most of the other figures are soberly clad in browns, greys and blues, except the young man taking snuff, fourth from the left, who is in azure blue, and the military figure, next to him but two, who is in scarlet. The seated boy is in brown on a red cushion and the standing boy in blue.

The paintings on the walls are not recognisable but the very large battle piece on the left looks as though it ought to be. It has been pointed out (Millar, 1963, p174) that the canvasses on the walls in this and in (50) are reminiscent of the French painters employed by the 1st Duke of Montagu at Montagu house.

The following suggestions have been made for the identity of the nobleman; Hawkins, 1776 (ed. 1963, p725), 'There is now in being a fine picture by the elder (sic) Laroon, of John, Duke of Marlborough at his levée, in which his Grace is represented dressed in a scarlet suit, with large white satin cuffs, and a very long white peruke, which he combs while his valet, who stands behind him, adjusts the curls after the comb has passed through them'; Southill catalogue of 1815, the Duke of Buckingham; Edwards, 1935, p196, possibly Frederick, Prince of Wales; Millar, 1951, p46, John, Duke of Montagu, 'The Knight of the Garter is like contemporary portraits of Montagu at Boughton and Hinchingbroke'.

Michael Sevier, the compiler of the catalogue to S. Sitwell's *Conversation Pieces*, mentions, on p103, 'the discovery in the British Museum of a sketch – – – representing the two figures on the extreme left'. This sketch cannot now be found.

Major Simon Whitbread,
Southill Park, Biggleswade

14 FÊTE GALANTE
c 1735   Plate 20

SIZE Probably about 36 × 28 in / 90 × 70 cm

MEDIUM Oil on canvas.

LITERATURE T. Borenius, 'The Kaleidoscope of Taste', *The Studio*, December 1931. Reproduction in colour from which the present illustration has been made.

NOTES In a wooded park-like landscape painted in dull browns and greens a sunset sky is seen through the trees. In the centre a woman in pink is singing to the accompaniment of an arch-lute played by a man standing behind her. To the left is a group conversing and drinking. To the right a young man in red kneels to kiss the hand of an elderly woman. Near her is an elderly man in slightly fantastic dress carrying flowers, and a country woman. Behind the balustrade of a terrace a young man in blue is talking to a woman in gold. They are being served with drinks by a red-headed page. A red macaw perches on the balustrade.

Destroyed by enemy action in 1940 when in the collection of Mrs Philip Trotter, who had owned it since before 1931.

15 COMMEDIA DELL' ARTE SCENE
c 1735   Fig 28

SIZE 36¼ × 34½ in / 92.1 × 87.6 cm

MEDIUM Oil on canvas.

PROVENANCE With Moore, London, about 1920; with Galerie Erhardt, Berlin; Heinrich Hirschberg, Berlin, as by Mercier; by descent to Mrs Ellen H. Wolfner, New York; with the Sabin Galleries, London, 1964 from whom bought by the present owners.

LITERATURE R. Raines, 'Marcellus Laroon and the Commedia dell'Arte', *The Art Quarterly* (Detroit) Summer 1962 pp108–112.

NOTES In a wooded park-like landscape with blue distance, a number of Commedia dell'Arte characters are giving an entertainment on a stone terrace. The Commedia figures are, from left to right, Scaramouche playing a guitar, two innamorati in blue and pink, Pierrot, Dottore in black and possibly a courtezan in blue, and Harlequin on the shoulders of a scowling Hercules. Other figures are a group seated on the ground on the left in blue, green and brown, two berobed figures of doubtful sex, a small fat man and a serving maid.

For discussion of this painting, which until 1962 was attributed to Philip Mercier, see pp70–72.

Mr & Mrs Paul Mellon,
Upperville, Virginia

16 OFFICER AND LADY AT SUPPER
c 1735   Plate 26

Mr & Mrs Paul Mellon,
Upperville, Virginia

SIZE 14⅜ × 12¼ in / 36.5 × 31 cm

MEDIUM Oil on canvas.

PROVENANCE Possibly one of the two paintings of a *Supper Party* exhibited at the Whitechapel Art Gallery 1906, nos. 146 and 150, both then in the possession of Mr and Mrs Martin H. Colnaghi; with M. Bernard, 1956.

EXHIBITIONS London, Blairman and Sons, *Marcellus Laroon*, 1951 (13); Richmond, Virginia, *Painting in England 1700–1850 – Collection of Mr and Mrs Paul Mellon*, 1963 (203).

NOTES The young woman is in a puce dress and on the back of her chair is a red cloak or wrap (?). The officer is in blue and behind him is a man servant in dull red carrying a tray with syllabub glasses.

17 THE BLACK PRINCE
c 1740   Plate 33

Collection unknown

SIZE 54 × 45½ in / 137.2 × 115.6 cm

MEDIUM Oil on canvas.

PROVENANCE Rev. Sir Hugh Smith-Marriott; Christie's, 17th January 1947 (114), as *Don Quixote with orderly in a wood*; with Arthur Tooth and Sons Ltd, 1949; with M. Bernard, 1955.

EXHIBITION London, Blairman and Sons, *Marcellus Laroon*, 1951 (9).

NOTES In a clearing in a dense wood, delicately painted in many shades of green, a knight in full armour on a white horse is gesturing to a pikeman.

The title of *The Black Prince*, which this painting has borne for some years is retained for convenience of reference, although the scene seems to have no likely connection with that historical figure, nor with Don Quixote (see pp67–8).

18 STAGE FIGURE
(Guy Fawkes)
c 1740   Plate 36

Private collection, England

SIZE 24½ × 16¾ in / 61.6 × 42.6 cm

MEDIUM Oil on canvas.

PROVENANCE (?Wm) Appleton collection according to a label on the back of the frame; Sir Osbert Sitwell since 1951.

NOTES A full-length figure of a man wearing a brown cloak and red breeches with sword and pistol in his belt is moving cautiously to his left. Although titled *Guido Fawkes* on a label on the back of the frame, the figure is more likely to represent some stage character.

19 LOVERS IN A PARK
c 1745   Fig 31

SIZE 24½ × 20¼ in / 63.3 × 50.4 cm

MEDIUM Oil on canvas.

PROVENANCE With the Howard Young Gallery, New York, 1927; Christie's, 19th July 1929 (95); with C. Duits; Tancred Borenius; Mme Borenius; with Thos. Agnew and Sons, 1956; R. H. Callaghan.

LITERATURE T. Borenius, 'The Kaleidoscope of Taste', *The Studio*, December 1931, reproduced in colour opposite p356.

EXHIBITIONS London, 25 Park Lane, *English Conversation Pieces*, 1930, (130); London, Blairman and Sons, *Marcellus Laroon*, 1951, (6); Richmond, Virginia, *Painting in England 1700–1850 – Collection of Mr and Mrs Paul Mellon*, 1963, (202); London, Royal Academy, *Painting in England 1700–1850*, 1964–5, (29).

Mr & Mrs Paul Mellon,
Upperville, Virginia

NOTES A young couple, he in black with red lined cloak, she in pink and white, walk along a path in a wooded park with a house in the left background.
  Seeing this painting again after some years, and after cleaning, has made me revise my former dating of about 1735 by some ten years (see pp72–4).

20 THE RENCONTRE
(Lady and Gentleman
in a Landscape)
c 1750   Plate 44

SIZE 36 × 24 in / 91.4 × 61 cm

MEDIUM Oil on canvas.

PROVENANCE With D. Lewis; Christie's, 12th March 1937 (49), as *Lovers in a Garden*; possibly with Davis Brothers; with M. Bernard.

LITERATURE *York Art Gallery Catalogue II*, 1963 (11).

EXHIBITION Dijon, *Peintures Anglaises des Collections d' York et Yorkshire*, 1957 (5).

NOTES The young woman wears a pale puce-coloured dress looped up to show her white petticoat embroidered with blue. She has white shoes with red heels and a white lace hat. The man wears a blue coat, white waistcoat and black breeches.

City Art Gallery, York

21 COUNTRY COUPLE WALKING

c 1750

Fig 50
? Eric Wood, Alkham, Kent

SIZE Oval 13 × 9½ in / 33 × 24.1 cm

MEDIUM Oil on panel.

PROVENANCE Christie's, 8th June 1923 (93), as *Lovers*, said to be inscribed on the back *from the Forman collection*. *A Conversation in an oval* was lot 150 in the sale of the collection of James, Duke of Chandos, on 8th March 1747. As no other oval picture by either of the Laroons is known it might be identical with this.

22 INTERIOR WITH FIGURES

c 1750   Plate 45

Tate Gallery, London (4420)

SIZE 17 × 15 in / 43 × 38 cm

MEDIUM Oil on canvas.

PROVENANCE L. H. McCormick; Christie's, 1st December 1922 (76), as *A Merry Party, a group of four (sic) ladies and gentlemen round a table*; Julian Lousada, by whom presented, through the N.A.C.F., to the Tate Gallery in 1928.

LITERATURE F. Antal, *Hogarth and his place in European Art*, 1962, p100.

NOTES From left to right there is a man in blue, a young woman in puce, a bawd in brown, a young woman in brown and a man in red. There are six figures including the servant, not four as in Christie's description.

23 A GENTLEMAN IN BROWN

c 1750   Plate 47

SIZE 34¼ × 27¾ in / 87 × 70.5 cm

MEDIUM Oil on canvas.

23 A GENTLEMAN IN BROWN *continued*

Michael Bevan,
Longstowe, Cambridgeshire

PROVENANCE With the Sackville Gallery, 1931; with H. A. Sutch, 1938; with Leggatt Brothers; Captain Richard Briscoe.

EXHIBITION London, Blairman and Sons, *Marcellus Laroon*, 1951 (4).

NOTES An informal half-length portrait of a young man in a brown coat and white waistcoat and stock. The background with its unrealistic sketchy trees suggests a stage backcloth.

24 LADY AND GENTLEMAN WITH A PAGE
c 1750–55   Plate 49

Edmund Naylor,
Barnet, Hertfordshire

SIZE 30 × 25 in / 76.2 × 63.5 cm

MEDIUM Oil on canvas.

PROVENANCE Lord Rowton of Rowton Castle, Shropshire; Christie's, 20th December 1902 (138), as by Hogarth; Lord Enfield; Countess of Strafford; by family descent to the present owner.

NOTES A man in a red military coat walks with a lady in a dark brown overdress. Her train is held by a page dressed in light brown. The dresses are elaborate and fanciful and are suggestive of stage costume.
   Probably a little reduced in size when it was relined, as the trees on the right and left appear cut off.

25 LOVERS IN A GLADE (II)
c 1750–55   Plate 51

Mr & Mrs Paul Mellon,
Upperville, Virginia

SIZE 35 × 27 in / 88.9 × 68.6 cm

MEDIUM Oil on canvas.

PROVENANCE Miss Lucas; Christie's, 18th June 1917 (126), and again 4th February 1924 (136), bought in at both sales; Sotheby's 10th July 1963 (146A); with Leger Gallery.

NOTES A man in brown and a woman in blue and white are sitting on a bank in a blueish-green landscape.
   The figures are smaller, in comparison with the landscape, than is usual with Laroon.

26 DANCERS AND MUSICIANS
c 1750/55   Fig 26

Private Collection, England

SIZE $34\frac{1}{2} \times 27\frac{1}{4}$ in / 87.6 × 69.1 cm

MEDIUM Oil on canvas.

PROVENANCE A. G. H. Ward; with H. A. Sutch; Sir Osbert Sitwell.

EXHIBITIONS London, 45 Park Lane, *Old London*, 1938, as *The Two Dancers*; London, Leicester Galleries, *The Dance*, 1938 (61), as *Masqueraders dancing on a stage*; London, Blairman and Sons, *Marcellus Laroon*, 1951 (8); London, Royal Academy, *English Taste in the Eighteenth Century*, 1955–6 (112).

NOTES Against a buff backcloth with pink decoration a woman in greenish-blue and a man in pink are dancing. Harlequin is in red, green and white chequering, and the double bass player in black.

27 A MUSICAL CONVERSATION (I)
c 1760   Plate 53

Duke of Buccleuch,
Boughton House

SIZE $27\frac{1}{4} \times 35$ in / 68.2 × 88.9 cm

MEDIUM Oil on canvas.

SIGNED *M.L.* on the cover of a book lying on the floor.

PROVENANCE Rev. J. E. Waldy.

LITERATURE R. Edwards, 'The Conversation Pictures of Marcellus Laroon (1679–1772)', *Apollo*, October 1935, p195; E. K. Waterhouse, *Painting in Britain 1530–1790*, (1953), p143.

EXHIBITIONS London, *National Portraits*, 1867 (359), as *George Brudenell, 4th E. of Cardigan and Lady Mary Montagu*; Leeds, *National Portraits*, 1868 (1096), as *The Marriage of the Duke of Montagu*; London, Blairman and Sons, *Marcellus Laroon*, 1951 (2).

NOTES Painted on a buff ground in muted tones of brown, blue, puce and red. The impasted brush-point highlights are prominent.

28 A MUSICAL CONVERSATION (II)
c 1760   Plate 54

SIZE $25\frac{1}{2} \times 30\frac{1}{4}$ in / 64.8 × 76.8 cm

MEDIUM Oil on canvas.

PROVENANCE Christie's, 26th April 1929 (23); with J. R. Saunders.

28 A MUSICAL CONVERSATION (II) *continued*

Lady Martin, London

LITERATURE S. Sitwell, *Conversation Pieces* (1936), p72.

EXHIBITIONS London, Blairman and Sons, *Marcellus Laroon*, 1951 (3); London, The Iveagh Bequest, Kenwood, *The Conversation Piece in Georgian England*, 1965 (29).

NOTES The colour scheme of muted tonality is much like (27).

29 A GALLANT CONVERSATION
c 1760

Fig 51

Present owner not known

SIZE Unknown, but probably quite small.

PROVENANCE With the Sackville Gallery, 1931.

LITERATURE T. Borenius, 'The Kaleidoscope of Taste', *The Studio*, 1931, p355.

NOTES Seated on a bank in a landscape a young man is declaring his love to a lady who has a small dog on her knee and a shepherd's crook in her left hand.

30 HORSEMAN AND FRUITSELLER
c 1760   Plate 55

Private collection, England

SIZE 20½ × 13 in / 52.0 × 33.0 cm

MEDIUM Oil on canvas.

PROVENANCE An inscription on the cross bar of the stretcher reads *Henry Launcelot Allen* (or possible *Alken*) *from his grandfather G. A. Lamb, 16th August 1864*; A. G. H. Ward; with H. A. Sutch; Sir Osbert Sitwell.

EXHIBITION London, Blairman and Sons, *Marcellus Laroon*, 1951 (11).

NOTES A young military man in red, riding a white horse, is handing a bag of money to a young woman in green walking beside him, who offers him an apple from a basket of fruit which she is holding.

31 LADY AND GENTLEMAN RIDING THROUGH A WOOD
c 1760   Plate 56

Private Collection, England

SIZE 21 × 12⅞ in / 53.3 × 32.7 cm

MEDIUM Oil on canvas.

PROVENANCE Sotheby's, 18th June 1952 (80).

NOTES A woman in a puce dress riding a white horse is followed by a man in blue on a brown horse.

32 LADY AND GENTLEMAN WITH A CRIPPLED BEGGAR
c 1760

Fig 52

SIZE 17½ × 14½ in / 44.5 × 36.9 cm

MEDIUM Oil on canvas.

INSCRIBED *Marcellus Laroon fecit* (in black paint on the verso).

PROVENANCE Mrs Morell, Black Hall, Oxford.

EXHIBITIONS London, 25 Park Lane, *English Conversation Pieces*, 1930 (111).

NOTES Destroyed by enemy action while in the collection of Thomas Girtin.

33 HORSEMAN STOPPING FOR WINE
c 1760   Plate 58

Sir Mordaunt Milner, Bt., Cape Town

SIZE 18 × 14¾ in / 45.7 × 37.5 cm

MEDIUM Oil on canvas.

PROVENANCE F. D. Lycett Green.

NOTES Sketchily painted with the rider in blue and the woman on a white horse with panniers.

34 THE BARBER'S SHOP
1760's   Plate 59

SIZE 17 × 13 in / 43.2 × 33.0 cm

MEDIUM Oil on canvas.

INSCRIBED Inscribed: *Oxford May ye 5 1770 I Gave This Picture to Mr Christopher Yeats* and in another hand *By Wm Hogarth*. (verso).

PROVENANCE As above; Christie's, 28th July 1938 (88); Sir Osbert Sitwell; G. F. Trumper.

EXHIBITIONS London, Blairman and Sons, *Marcellus Laroon*, 1951 (10).

Miss G. M. Trumper, London

NOTES The inscription may imply that the picture was painted in 1770.

35 THE SONG
1760's   Plate 60

SIZE 13⅛ × 10¼ in / 33.3 × 26.0 cm

MEDIUM Oil on canvas.

PROVENANCE A. G. H. Ward; with Leggatt Brothers; Captain Richard Briscoe.

Michael Bevan,
Longstowe, Cambridgeshire

EXHIBITION London, Blairman and Sons, *Marcellus Laroon*, 1951 (12).

36 YOUNG MAN IN A TAVERN
1760's   Plate 62

SIZE 14 5/16 × 12¼ in / 36.4 × 29.3 cm

MEDIUM Oil on canvas.

PROVENANCE With M. Bernard, 1965; Bonham's 14th October 1965 (73); with Saunders, Oxford.

NOTES The young man wears a blue coat and sits on a red-upholstered chair. The serving man is in brown.

Collection unknown

**37 A MARKET TENT
    IN CAMP**
    (Soldiers making merry)
    1707   Fig 16

SIZE $11\frac{1}{2} \times 15\frac{7}{8}$ in / 29.1 × 40.4 cm

MEDIUM Pencil.

SIGNED AND DATED *Mar Laroon F 1707.* The signature and date have been inked over but appear to be unaltered.

INSCRIBED *In Flanders. a Market Tent in Camp* (recto). *Done in Flanders in the year 1707, the year I went into the Army. Mar Laroon.* (verso).

PROVENANCE Richard Redgrave; Sotheby's 29th June 1932 (121); with B. Squire; L. G. Duke; Sir Robert Witt, by whom bequeathed to the Courtauld Institute in 1952.

University of London, Courtauld
Institute of Art – Witt Collection
(2709)

EXHIBITIONS London, Chesterfield House, *Marlborough and the Reign of Queen Anne,* 1934 (504); London, Blairman and Sons, *Marcellus Laroon,* 1951, (C).

**38 EXECUTION OF
    DESERTERS**
    1707   Fig 15

SIZE $7\frac{1}{2} \times 10\frac{7}{8}$ in / 19 × 27.6 cm

MEDIUM Black and brown inks on pencil.

INSCRIBED *at Meldert Camp. 1707 Execution of Deserters in Flanders. 1707.*

PROVENANCE With Christopher Gibbs, 1963.

NOTES To the right of the gallows and behind the two soldiers a clergyman can be seen giving the last rites. This spontaneous sketch may have been inked in later, and the two figures on the right added. Marlborough's headquarters were at Meldert 1706–7.

John Richardson, London

39 Mr ROLUS
    portrait studies of John Rollos
    1718

SIZE $12\frac{3}{8} \times 7\frac{3}{4}$ in / 31.6 × 19.9 cm

MEDIUM Pencil.

INSCRIBED *Mr. Rolus his Majestys Engraver of ye broad seal 1718.*

PROVENANCE Horace Walpole; Robins (Strawberry Hill sale) 23rd June 1842 (1252), one of eleven drawings 'by Marcellus Laroon, chiefly pencil sketches of very remarkable characters, taken about the year 1725, amongst which are two sketches of Mr Rolus, engraver of the broad seal to King George I', bought by Burn; Edward Daniell from whom bought by the British Museum in 1876.

LITERATURE L. Binyon, *Catalogue of Drawings by British Artists . . . in the British Museum, vol. III,* p36, no. 2.

Fig 53
British Museum – Department of
Prints and Drawings (1876–7–8–2390)
London.

EXHIBITION British Museum, *William Hogarth*, 1964 (55).

NOTES The two heads are doubtfully of the same sitter, but I have not found another portrait of John Rollos with which to compare them. The profile resembles a medallion head.

---

40 **A DINNER PARTY**
1719 Plate 4

P. D. Matthiesen, London

SIZE $11\frac{1}{2} \times 9\frac{7}{8}$ in / 29.2 × 25 cm

MEDIUM Pen and brown ink.

SIGNED AND DATED *M. Laroon fecit 1719*.

INSCRIBED *Presented to King George Ist a picture I painted in 1725* and *Premiere pensee*.

PROVENANCE From 'a French collection'; F. Matthiesen

EXHIBITION London, Royal Academy, *European Masters of the Eighteenth Century*, 1954–5 (602).

NOTES This is a preliminary sketch for the *Dinner Party* (1), its relationship to the painting being discussed on p77.

41 **ALMS MEN**
1720 Fig 38

SIZE $11\frac{1}{4} \times 14\frac{3}{8}$ in / 28.6 × 36.5 cm

MEDIUM Pencil.

SIGNED AND DATED *M.L.F. 1720.*

INSCRIBED *Alms men.*

National Gallery of Scotland
Edinburgh; Department of Prints and
Drawings (RN 1333)

PROVENANCE David Laing, LL.D., who bequeathed it to the Royal Scottish Academy in 1879, who, in turn, presented it to the National Gallery of Scotland in 1910.

42 **MAN HOLDING A BOOK**
1724 Plate 7

SIZE $7\frac{5}{8} \times 6$ in / 19.4 × 14.3 cm

MEDIUM Pencil.

SIGNED AND DATED *M. Laroon Fecit 1724.*

PROVENANCE With Yvonne ffrench from whom bought by the present owner in 1961.

L. G. Duke, London

NOTES On the left below a (?) bookcase is a partly illegible inscription, which appears to read *C.F.C Pe – – – (?) Bt.*

43 **A LADY AND
GENTLEMAN AT TEA**
1729 Plate 8

SIZE $12\frac{1}{8} \times 7\frac{7}{8}$ in / 30.8 × 20 cm

MEDIUM Pencil.

SIGNED AND DATED *M. Laroon Fecit 1729.* This signature, partly erased, can be seen under a most inexpertly forged *W. Hogarth.* The ink line does not follow the contours of the pencil line of the date which appears, however, to be the same *1729.* Stylistically this date is correct. There are faint signs of an erased inscription alongside the signature.

PROVENANCE Sir Edward Marsh; by whom bequeathed, through the National Art Collections Fund, to Edinburgh.

National Gallery of Scotland
Edinburgh; Department of Prints and
Drawings

EXHIBITIONS London, Whitechapel Art Gallery, 1906 (14); London, Royal Academy, *British Art,* 1934 (1111), as a doubtful Hogarth; London, Blairman and Sons, *Marcellus Laroon,* 1951 (D).

44 MUSIC PARTY (Ia)
1731   Plate 10

Paul Walraf, London

SIZE $14\frac{3}{4} \times 12$ in / 37.5 × 30.5 cm

MEDIUM Pencil.

SIGNED AND DATED *Marcellus Laroon Fecit. 1731*. An attempt has been made to alter the date to *1701*.

PROVENANCE Possibly Stephano Carbonelli; Sir Robert Witt; with Peter Claas in 1964 from whom bought by the present owner.

NOTES This may be the finished drawing (see no. 45) for Stephano Carbonelli, as its dimensions are much the same as the other finished drawings (nos. 50, 53, 54, 55), but whereas they are in pen over pencil this is in pencil alone.

45 MUSIC PARTY (Ib)
1731

Fig 54
Collection unknown

SIZE $8\frac{1}{2} \times 7\frac{1}{2}$ in / 21.5 × 19 cm

MEDIUM Pencil.

INSCRIBED *made a finished Drawing of this for Mr Carbonelli 1731*.

PROVENANCE Paris, Drouot, Bourgarel sale, 15th June 1922 (63), as *Musique du Chambre*.

NOTES This is the sketch for (44).

46 A FARMER PUTTING HIS SON APPRENTICE TO AN ATTORNEY
1731   Plate 13

SIZE $13\frac{1}{8} \times 18\frac{3}{4}$ in / 33.3 × 47.6 cm

MEDIUM Pencil.

SIGNED AND DATED *Mar: Laroon fecit 1731*.

INSCRIBED *a Farmer putting his Son apprentice to an Attorney*.

PROVENANCE Acquired by the Gallery in 1920, possibly from Agnew's of Manchester.

46 A FARMER PUTTING HIS SON APPRENTICE TO AN ATTORNEY *continued*

Whitworth Art Gallery, Manchester

NOTES On the right the farmer, holding a bag of money, and his wife listen to the attorney reading from a document. To the left a man, wearing Geneva bands and with a paper in his pocket marked 'Tythes' so presumably a clergyman, discusses a document with another man.

---

47 SCENE IN A GARDEN
(A Pinch of Snuff)
1732   Plate 15

SIZE $16\frac{1}{8} \times 11\frac{11}{16}$ in / 40.8 × 29.7 cm

MEDIUM Pencil.

SIGNED AND DATED *Mar. Laroon F. 1732*. An attempt has been made to alter the date to 1702, and the signature has been pencilled over.

PROVENANCE Richard Bull; Bull sale, Sotheby's, 23rd May 1881 (77); where bought by the British Museum through A. W. Thibaudeau.

LITERATURE L. Binyon, *Catalogue of Drawings by British Artists . . . in the British Museum*, vol. III, p36, no. 3; R. Davies, *Chats on Old English Drawings* (1923), p76.

EXHIBITION London, British Museum, *William Hogarth*, 1964 (54).

British Museum Department of Prints and Drawings (1881–6–11–166), London

NOTES There is perhaps some later pencil work on parts of this drawing, notably on the trees on the right and on the faces.

---

48 GROUP OF FIGURES AT A TABLE (I)
(A New Years Party)
1732/3   Plate 11

SIZE $7\frac{1}{2} \times 9\frac{3}{4}$ in / 19 × 24.7 cm

MEDIUM Pencil.

SIGNED AND DATED *M. Laroon F 1732/3*.

INSCRIBED *Designed for Mr. Mat: Ashton*.

PROVENANCE Matthew Ashton; Sir Robert Witt by whom bequeathed to the Courtauld Institute in 1952.

University of London,
Courtauld Institute of Art
Witt Collection (682)

LITERATURE R. Davies, *Chats on Old English Drawings* (1923), p76.

49 GROUP OF FIGURES AT A TABLE (II)
1732/3   Plate 12

SIZE $7\frac{7}{8} \times 9\frac{3}{4}$ in / 20 × 24.9 cm

MEDIUM Pencil.

SIGNED AND DATED *Mar. Laroon F. 1732/3.*

INSCRIBED *Designed for Mr: Mat. Ashton.*

PROVENANCE Matthew Ashton; Sir Robert Witt; with Colnaghi's.

LITERATURE R. Davies, *Chats on Old English Drawings* (1923), p76.

EXHIBITION Paris, Musée des Arts Decoratifs, *Caricatures et moeurs anglaises*, 1928 (69), as *Drinking Party.*

John Bryson, Oxford

NOTES A group similar to no. 48 but with eleven figures.

50 MUSIC PARTY (IIa)
1733

Fig 55
Fitzwilliam Museum, Cambridge
(P.D. 2–1947)

SIZE $13\frac{1}{2} \times 10\frac{1}{2}$ in / 34.3 × 26.7 cm

MEDIUM Pen and ink over pencil with wash.

SIGNED AND DATED *Mar: Laroon Dux. Fecit. 1733.*

PROVENANCE Bendall Martyn; Randall Davies; Davies sale, Sotheby's, 11th February 1947 (267), as *Party at Montagu House*; with Colnaghi's; given to the Museum by the Friends of the Fitzwilliam in 1947.

LITERATURE R. Davies, *Chats on Old English Drawings* (1923), p76.

NOTES On the wall is a large Laroon-like picture of the Judgement of Paris. This is the finished drawing for Bendall Martyn (51).

51 MUSIC PARTY (IIb)
1733   Plate 18

SIZE $10\frac{5}{8} \times 8\frac{1}{4}$ in / 27 × 21 cm

MEDIUM Pencil.

51   MUSIC PARTY (IIb) *continued*

INSCRIBED *The finishd Drawing for Mr. Bendall Martyn : Secretary to the Excise : 1733.*

PROVENANCE Christie's, 18th July 1947 (42), as *The Tea Party*; with Spink and Son; with Colnaghi's; Clifford Duits; Sir Bruce Ingram.

EXHIBITION London, Blairman and Sons, *Marcellus Laroon*, 1951 (not in catalogue).

Henry E. Huntington Library and
Art Gallery, San Marino, California

NOTES This sketch for (50) has only minor differences.

---

52   **RIDERS AND BEGGARS**
    1735   Plate 21

SIZE 18¼ × 13 in / 47 × 33 cm

MEDIUM Pen and ink over pencil with brown wash.

SIGNED AND DATED *Marcellus Laroon* (erasure) *Fecit. 1735.*

LITERATURE A. P. Oppé, *English Drawings, Stuart and Georgian Periods at Windsor Castle* (1950) p71, No 410.

HM The Queen, Windsor Castle,
(Windsor Inventory 13308)

NOTES On the left a young woman on horseback, who could easily be mistaken for a man, offers snuff to a young man also mounted.

---

53   **MUSIC PARTY (III)**
    1735   Plate 22

SIZE 15½ × 11 in / 39.3 × 27.9 cm

MEDIUM Pen and ink over pencil with wash.

SIGNED AND DATED *Mar : Laroon. Fecit. 1735.*

PROVENANCE Mendelssohn-Bartholdy; Sir Robert Witt by whom bequeathed to the Courtauld Institute in 1952.

LITERATURE Thieme Becker, vol. 22, p390.

EXHIBITIONS London, Victoria and Albert Museum, *Drawings – – – from the Collection of Sir Robert Witt*, 1943; London, Blairman and Sons, *Marcellus Laroon*, 1951 (F); Arts Council, *Three Centuries of British Watercolours and Drawings*, 1951 (103), and *Drawings from the Witt Collection*, 1953 (20).

University of London,
Courtauld Institute of Art
Witt Collection (3256)

NOTES This is a 'finished drawing', but the sketch, which would probably be inscribed with the recipient's name, is not known.

54 MUSIC PARTY (IV)
1735   Plate 23

SIZE $17\frac{3}{4} \times 13$ in $/45.1 \times 33$ cm

MEDIUM Pen and ink over pencil with wash.

SIGNED AND DATED *Marcellus Laroon. Dux. Fecit. 1735.*

PROVENANCE Richard Redgrave; Sotheby's, 29th June 1932 (122); with B. Squire; J. Leslie Wright.

EXHIBITION London, Royal Academy, *Masters of British Watercolour – J. Leslie Wright Collection*, 1949 (6).

City Museum and Art Gallery, Birmingham

NOTES This is another 'finished drawing' for which the sketch is missing.

55 MUSIC PARTY (Va)
1736   Plate 24

SIZE $17\frac{7}{8} \times 13\frac{1}{8}$ in $/45.3 \times 33.4$ cm

MEDIUM Pen and ink over pencil with wash.

SIGNED AND DATED *Marcellus. Laroon. Fecit. 1736.*

PROVENANCE Horace Walpole (*A Description of Strawberry Hill*, 1784, p91 'in the Passage', near the Great Bedchamber); Strawberry Hill sale, 17th May 1842 (121), *A drawing of a Concert, by Captain Laroon*; with J. W. B. Tiffin from whom bought by the Museum in 1848.

LITERATURE L. Binyon, *Catalogue of Drawings by British Artists . . . in the British Museum*, vol. III p36, no. 4; R. Davies, *Chats on Old English Drawings* (1923), p76; R. Edwards, 'The Conversation Pictures of Marcellus Laroon' (1679–1772), *Apollo*, October 1935, p193; S. Sitwell, *Conversation Pieces* (1936), p71.

EXHIBITION London, British Museum, *William Hogarth*, 1964 (51).

NOTES On the right a man, closely resembling John James Heidegger, is playing a harpsichord.
    This drawing was inscribed by Horace Walpole: *A Concert by Captain Laroon. The gentleman on the left under the door is John, 2nd Duke of Montagu; the Lady standing by him is his 2nd Daughter, Mary Countess of Cardigan, afterwards Duchess of Montagu. H.W.*
    This inscription, which must have been written at least thirty years after the date of the drawing as the Dukedom of Montagu was not conferred on the Earl of Cardigan until 1766, is responsible for a number of Laroon's paintings and drawings being connected, quite erroneously in my opinion, with the Montagu family. For further comments on this problem see p80.

British Museum, London
Department of Prints and Drawings
(1848–7–8–207)

56 A FRENCHMAN AT BOW STREET (correctly, Night Walkers before a Justice)
1740 Plate 31

SIZE 14⅛ × 20½ in / 36.2 × 51.8 cm

MEDIUM Pencil.

SIGNED AND DATED *M : Laroon. F : 1740.*

PROVENANCE Probably lot 90, 'drawings framed and glazed', in the sale of Samuel Scott's collection on 13th January 1773, *Capt. Laroon A Night Scene, with figures appearing before a justice*; the Prince Regent who bought it from Colnaghi on 18th January 1813 (archives invoice 27911).

LITERATURE A. P. Oppé, *English Drawings, Stuart and Georgian Periods, at Windsor Castle* (1950), pp14, 71. No. 409.

NOTES On the left the justice is seated in front of a table where his clerk is writing, while in the centre is a man apparently pleading with the justice. More than twenty other figures including prisoners, tipstaves and onlookers, provide a scene of great animation.

It is inscribed in the lower margin: *A Curious and Interesting Drawing by Laroon of a French Gentn Brought at night before the Justice at Bow S–*, in the hand which Oppé recognised as that of a member of the Colnaghi firm who inscribed a number of drawings now in the Royal Collection. There seems little doubt that the inscription was added at the time of the sale to the Prince Regent in 1813. The recently discovered sketch (93), for (56), gives Laroon's title *Night Walkers before a Justice*, but *A Frenchman at Bow Street* has been retained here as it is referred to by this title in the Windsor inventory and in Oppé's catalogue.

HM The Queen, Windsor Castle, (Windsor Castle Inventory 13309)

57 ROCKY LANDSCAPE WITH FIGURES
1743 Plate 38

SIZE 13½ × 10¹⁵⁄₁₆ in / 34.3 × 27.8 cm

MEDIUM Pencil and brown wash.

SIGNED AND DATED *M : Laroon F. 1743.* The date has been partly inked over and the third figure changed to *o*. The underlying *4* can be seen on careful examination.

PROVENANCE Possibly lot 92 in the sale of Samuel Scott's collection on 13th January 1773, *A drawing framed and glazed of an upright landscape with figures*; Randall Davies; Leslie Wright; with Colnaghi's; Mrs B. K. Young; Sir Robert Witt, by whom bequeathed to the Courtauld Institute in 1952.

EXHIBITIONS London, Royal Academy, *British Art*, 1934 (1115); London, Blairman and Sons, *Marcellus Laroon*, 1951 (A).

University of London,
Courtauld Institute of Art
Witt Collection (3996)

**58 PROMENADE IN
THE MALL**
1744   Plate 37

SIZE $15\frac{5}{8} \times 11\frac{7}{8}$ in / 39.7 × 30.2 cm

MEDIUM Pen and ink over pencil with wash.

SIGNED AND DATED *Mar: Laroon. F. 1744.*

PROVENANCE With W. B. Tiffin from whom purchased by the Museum in 1854.

LITERATURE L. Binyon, *Catalogue of Drawings by British Artists . . . in the British Museum,* vol. III p36, no. 5; R. Davies, *Chats on Old English Drawings* (1923), p76.

British Museum, London
Department of Prints and Drawings
(1854–8–12–146)

EXHIBITIONS London, British Museum, *William Hogarth*, 1964 (52).

NOTES St. James's Palace is seen in the background.

59 FIGURES WALKING
1744   Plate 39

SIZE $16\frac{3}{4} \times 13\frac{1}{4}$ in / 42.5 × 33.8 cm

MEDIUM Pen and ink over pencil.

SIGNED AND DATED *Marcellus Laroon F. 1744.*

PROVENANCE With Colnaghi's in 1961 from whom bought by the present owners.

EXHIBITIONS Richmond, Virginia, *Painting in England 1700–1850 – Collection of Mr and Mrs Paul Mellon*, 1963 (396).

NOTES The figures on the right have been inked over. The ink line is a little unlike Laroon's in the hatching which is more mechanical and especially in the hard outline of the face of the woman on the right, who can be compared with the almost identical figure in no. 58. There is a partly illegible inscription not in Laroon's hand, under the signature, which includes the words 'died in 1772', and must therefore be a biographical note.

Mr & Mrs Paul Mellon,
Upperville, Virginia

**60 THE WOODMAN
(Illustration to a story)**
1748   Plate 40

SIZE $8\frac{7}{8} \times 6\frac{11}{16}$ in / 22.9 × 17.3 cm

MEDIUM Pen and ink over pencil with wash.

SIGNED AND DATED *Mar: Laroon. F. 1748.*

LITERATURE L. Binyon, *Catalogue of Drawings by British Artists . . . in the British Museum,* vol. III p35, no. 1.

British Museum, London
Department of Prints and Drawings
(1857–6–13–1008), previously in the
Department of MSS.

NOTES A similar scene to (7) but with many differences.

61 LOVERS IN A GLADE (III)
1759   Plate 50

Basil Taylor, West Farleigh

SIZE 13⅜ × 10 3/16 in / 33.0 × 26.2 cm

MEDIUM Pencil.

SIGNED AND DATED *M.L.F. 1759.*

NOTES The young man's right foot has been redrawn in a different position.

**62 A GERMAN.
A FRENCH MAN**
1762   Plate 61

Seymour Slive, Cambridge, Mass.

SIZE 9⅝ × 13 in / 24.4 × 33.0 cm

MEDIUM Pencil and watercolour heightened with white.

SIGNED AND DATED *Mar: Laroon. F. 1762.*

INSCRIBED *a German. a French man.*

NOTES Two rather more than head and shoulders drawings of, on the left, a German, wearing a three cornered hat, hair in a queue, with his left hand on the hilt of a sword, and on the right, a French man with a braided hat and solitaire bow.

The photograph, which Professor Slive kindly sent me, of this lively drawing, suggests that it might be rather earlier, perhaps ten years or so, than the inscribed date, but without seeing the drawing it is impossible to form a definite opinion.

**63 COUNTRYMAN AND
APPLESELLER**
(Woman selling apples)
1764

Fig 56
John Ehrman, London

SIZE 12½ × 8⅜ in / 31.8 × 10.3 cm

MEDIUM Red chalk with pencil.

SIGNED AND DATED *M. Laroon F. 1764.*

PROVENANCE With Spink & Son Ltd, 1955.

NOTES There is an inscription in an old hand in the lower margin: *Was this by a son of Marcellus Lauron or Laroon famous for his Conversation Pieces – ̣– – 1705.* The drawing has been torn, repaired and laid down, and some of the inscription is illegible.

64 CHARITY
1770   Plate 67

SIZE 16 × 24½ in / 40.6 × 62.2 cm

MEDIUM Reed pen and brown ink over pencil with wash.

SIGNED AND DATED *Aetatis 92 Marcellus Laroon F. 1770.*

INSCRIBED *Charity.*

PROVENANCE Francis Douce by whom bequeathed to the Ashmolean in 1834. Douce acquired '2 drawings by Laroon' in July 1826 (Douce MS. e.68 – diary of purchases – in the Bodleian Library; the typescript, also in the Bodleian, gives the name as Larvon but there is no doubt that it is Laroon in the MS.). The two drawings are probably this and no. 65, but see also no. 103. There is no other mention of Laroon in Douce's diary of purchases which extends from 1804 to 1834.

NOTES The close relation to the hospital scene in Callot's *Les Petites Misères de la Guerre* is mentioned on p86.

Ashmolean Museum, Oxford

65 CUDGELING
1770   Plate 66

SIZE 18⅜ × 27¾ in / 46.7 × 70.5 cm

MEDIUM Reed pen and brown ink over pencil with wash.

SIGNED AND DATED *Aetatis 92. Marcellus Laroon F. 1770.*

INSCRIBED *Cudgeling.*

PROVENANCE As (64).

NOTES For a recent note on the relationship between cudgeling, backsword and singlestick, see J. Eyles, 'Backsword or Singlestick?' *Country Life*, 8th July 1965, p108. See also text p86.

Ashmolean Museum, Oxford

66 THE MORNING RIDE
1770   Plate 70

SIZE 14 × 11 in / 35.6 × 28 cm

MEDIUM Reed pen and brown ink over pencil with wash.

SIGNED AND DATED *Mar. Laroon F. 1770.*

PROVENANCE Viscount Knutsford; Sotheby's, 11th April 1935 (117); with B. Squire; with Colnaghi's, 1947; Gilbert Davis.

EXHIBITION Arts Council *British Water Colours and Drawings from the Gilbert Davis Collection*, 1949 (1).

Huntington Library and Art Gallery, San Marino, California

67 WOMAN AND CHILD
(Little Girl carrying her dog
and walking with her nurse)
1770

Fig 57
H. C. Torbock, Penrith,
Cumberland

**68 CAVALRYMEN ON THE
MARCH**
(Soldiers on horseback)
1771   Plate 72

University of London,
Courtauld Institute of Art
Witt Collection (2853)

69 A HUNTING PARTY
1771   Plate 73

Tate Gallery, London (3624)

SIZE 13½ × 8½ in / 34.3 × 21.6 cm

MEDIUM Ink over pencil.

SIGNED AND DATED *Mar. Laroon F. 1770.*

PROVENANCE Viscount Knutsford; Sotheby's, 11th April 1935 (118); with B. Squire; with Colnaghi's.

SIZE 18⅞ × 12¾ in / 47.9 × 32.4 cm

MEDIUM Reed pen and brown ink over pencil with wash.

SIGNED AND DATED *Marcellus. Laroon. F. 1771.*

PROVENANCE With Colnaghi's 1936; Sir Robert Witt by whom bequeathed to the Courtauld Institute in 1952.

LITERATURE S. Sitwell, *Conversation Pieces* (1936), p42.

EXHIBITIONS London, Blairman and Sons, *Marcellus Laroon*, 1951 (1); Arts Council, *Drawings from the Witt Collection*, 1953 (21).

SIZE 19¼ × 13 in / 49.1 × 33 cm

MEDIUM Reed pen and brown ink over pencil with wash.

SIGNED AND DATED *Mar. Laroon F. 1771.*

PROVENANCE H. S. Reitlinger, by whom presented to the Tate Gallery through the N.A.C.F. in 1922.

EXHIBITION CEMA touring exhibition, 1944 (41).

70 A HIGH WIND
1771 Plate 71

University of London,
Courtauld Institute of Art
Witt Collection (3602)

SIZE 20 11/16 × 30 13/16 in / 52.2 × 78.3 cm

MEDIUM Reed pen and brown and grey ink over pencil with wash.

SIGNED AND DATED *Aetat 92. Marcellus Laroon. F. 1771.*

INSCRIBED *a high Wind.*

PROVENANCE Sir Robert Witt by whom bequeathed to the Courtauld Institute in 1952.

EXHIBITION London, Blairman and Sons, *Marcellus Laroon*, 1951 (H).

71 A YOUNG GIRL
1771

Fig 58
Collection unknown

SIZE 7 × 5 in / 17.8 × 12.7 cm

MEDIUM Pen and ink.

SIGNED AND DATED *Mar. Laroon F. 1771.*

PROVENANCE H. Marcus Allen; Sotheby's, 25th February 1927 (120).

72 STREET SCENE
1772 Plate 74

Private collection, England

SIZE 18 3/4 × 12 1/2 in / 47.7 × 31.8 cm

MEDIUM Reed pen and brown ink over pencil with wash.

SIGNED AND DATED *Mar. Laroon. F. 1772.*

PROVENANCE Sir Osbert Sitwell.

EXHIBITIONS London, Magnasco Society, July 1927 (40), as *A State coach and horses*, the date given incorrectly as 1712; London, Blairman and Sons, *Marcellus Laroon*, 1951 (J); Royal Academy, *Old Master Drawings*, 1953 (222).

73 HEAD OF A SPANIARD
before 1700

Fig 59

Mr & Mrs Paul Mellon,
Upperville, Virginia

SIZE 4 7/16 × 2 7/8 in / 11.6 × 7.3 cm

MEDIUM Pen and brown wash over pencil.

SIGNED *M. Laroon. F.*

INSCRIBED *Spaniard.*

PROVENANCE With Colnaghi's 1963.

74 HEAD OF A TURK
before 1700

Fig 60

Mr & Mrs Paul Mellon,
Upperville, Virginia

SIZE 4 7/16 × 2 7/8 in / 11.6 × 7.3 cm

MEDIUM Pen and brown ink over pencil.

SIGNED *M. Laroon. F.*

INSCRIBED *Turk.*

PROVENANCE With Colnaghi's 1963.

75 HEAD OF A MAN
(Probably Marcellus Lauron)
before 1700

Fig 61

Mr & Mrs Paul Mellon,
Upperville, Virginia

SIZE $4\frac{1}{16} \times 3\frac{1}{16}$ in / 10.3 × 7.8 cm

MEDIUM Pen and brown ink over pencil.

INSCRIBED *Maroon's best Virginia London* (on hat).

PROVENANCE With Miss Yvonne ffrench 1964.

NOTES From the inscription it seems likely that this is a sketch of Lauron. For a further note on this and (73) and (74) see p57.

76 GROTESQUE MUSICIANS
c 1700   Plate 1

L. G. Duke, London

SIZE $8\frac{11}{16} \times 12\frac{3}{4}$ in / 22.1 × 32.4 cm

MEDIUM Pencil and monochrome wash, squared.

INSCRIBED *Grotesq drawing of fiddlers by Laroon* (an inscription, probably contemporary, on the old mount).

PROVENANCE Has the mark *E.P.* of Edmund Prideaux who died in 1745; with Colnaghi's, 1961, from whom bought by the present owner.

NOTES A group of seven men, several of them caricatured, of whom two are singing and others playing violin, one-stringed fiddle, descant shawm and unrecognisable instruments. The subject and figures can be compared with *The Execrable Concert*, (104).

77 BROKEN ON THE WHEEL
c 1710   Plate 2

I. R. C. Batchelor, Dundee

SIZE $11\frac{1}{8} \times 8\frac{5}{8}$ in / 28.3 × 21.9 cm

MEDIUM Pencil.

SIGNED *M.L.F.*

PROVENANCE E. H. Coles; Oliver Millar.

78 A PARK KEEPER
C 1710

Fig 62

Michael Bevan,
Longstowe, Cambridgeshire

SIZE 14½ × 11½ in / 36.8 × 29.2 cm

MEDIUM Pencil.

INSCRIBED *A Park Keepers Dress when he attacks Dear Stealers by ye life by M. Laroon.* (in Laroon's hand).

PROVENANCE Richard Bull; Bull sale, Sotheby's, 23rd May 1881 (73); probably with Carfax and Company, 1906; with Agnew's 1939; with Leggatt Bros; Captain Richard Briscoe.

EXHIBITIONS Probably Whitechapel Art Gallery Spring Exhibition 1906 (33) *A Park Keeper*, then with Carfax and Co.

79 LAROON AND REISEN
before 1725

Fig 63

Lord Methuen,
Corsham Court, Wiltshire

SIZE 8⅜ × 12¼ in / 21.3 × 31.1 cm

MEDIUM Pencil.

INSCRIBED *A Journey to Windsor by Capt Laroon & Mr. Christian ye Grav* (– –) and in balloons from the mouths of the two riders: *Keep yr Spurrs out of ye horses sides Christian and D-n ye horse.*

NOTES A caricature drawing showing two horsemen in some difficulty. The *Christian* must be Charles Christian Reisen, the gem engraver, (1680–1725), a fellow member with Laroon of both Kneller's Academy and the Rose and Crown Club. His portrait, according to Vertue, was drawn by John Laroon. I have had slight doubts about Laroon's authorship but the inscription is in his hand. The name of John Vanderbank occurs as a possible alternative.

On the verso are two caricature figures: on the left a full-length profile of a man with a long columnar neck and on the right a man seen full-length from the back. The latter is reminiscent of caricature drawings by Venetian artists such as Marco Ricci and Antonio Maria Zanetti. Neither is by Laroon but below is an inscription in his hand: under the left hand figure (?) *D. Preston by Mr* (– – –) and under the right hand *Moses Vanderbank in Mourning Drawn by himself.*

80 MAT ASHTON AT CHESTER
(A painter with three mocking figures) and BAJAZETT
before 1725   Plate 6

SIZE 8¾ × 12⅞ in / 22.3 × 32.8 cm

MEDIUM Pencil.

SIGNED *M. Lar. F.*

INSCRIBED *Mat Ashton the Painter at Chester. – Carigatura.* This inscription appears to be in Laroon's hand roughly pencilled over. In a balloon from Ashton's mouth is 'miserable Goths' but a remark from another figure has been completely erased.

PROVENANCE An inscription on the old mount reads: *Mr Bull found this drawing in a lot bought for him, some little time since: it may possibly be of some use to Mr Walpole, 'tis of none at all to Mr Bull, nor did he know 'till yesterday that it was in the Lot order'd to be bought for him. Friday 28, 1790;.* Francis Wellesley, no. 135 in the privately printed catalogue; Francis Wellesley sale, Sotheby's, 28th June, 1920 et seq. 3rd day (505); Randall Davies; Davies sale, Sotheby's, 11th Feb 1947 (266) as *Miserable Goths*, sold with No 107 in this catalogue; with Colnaghi's; Sir Robert Witt, by whom bequeathed to the Courtauld Institute in 1952.

EXHIBITIONS London, Blairman and Sons, *Marcellus Laroon*, 1951 (G).

NOTES Three men on the left are jeering at a fourth, presumably Ashton, who cuts an odd figure in a coat and boots too big for him and a wide-brimmed hat. Matthew Ashton was a portrait painter, working between 1725 and 1750 in London and Ireland. A member of the Rose and Crown Club, known as Teague presumably because of his Irish associations, he owned two drawings by Laroon (48), (49).

On the upper half of the verso, occupying about 8 by 6 in., is a pencil sketch by Laroon of the head and shoulders of a man at a table, the whole enveloped in an inverted cage or basket, with underneath the one word *Bajazett*. This may be a drawing of Alexander Nisbet (1675–1725), the heraldic writer and landscape painter and member of the Rose and Crown Club, one of whose names, according to Vertue, was Bajazet. Nisbet was also a member of the St. Martin's Lane Academy and probably identical with the 'Mr Nesbit-landskip' in Vertue's list of new subscribers to Kneller's Academy in 1713. Bajazet, the Turkish Emperor who was confined in a cage by his conqueror, Tamerlane, figures in a play by Nicholas Rowe and in an opera by Handel, both performed in London in the 1720s and 1730s. Above is a profile head similar to those in (81).

University of London,
Courtauld Institute of Art
Witt Collection (4348)

81 CARICATURE HEADS
before 1725

Fig 64

British Museum, London
Department of Prints and Drawings
(Cracherode G.g.1 – 469)

SIZE 7 × 9¾ in / 19.8 × 24.8 cm

MEDIUM Pencil.

PROVENANCE Rev. C. M. Cracherode by whom bequeathed to the Museum in 1799.

EXHIBITION London, British Museum, *William Hogarth*, 1964 (73).

NOTES Of eight separate profile heads, two are drawn as architectural capitals. There are two straight capitals on the right.

82 A DUTCHMAN AND HIS WIFE
1730's   Plate 16

SIZE $15\frac{1}{4} \times 11\frac{1}{2}$ in / 38.7 × 29.5 cm

MEDIUM Pencil and black chalk.

SIGNED AND DATED *Mar. Laroon F. 1702.*

INSCRIBED *a Dutchman and his Wife.* (in Laroon's hand).

PROVENANCE Probably identical with *La Promenade*, pencil, 41 by 30 cm, signed and dated 1702, lot 169 in the sale of drawings belonging to J. M. Vreeswijk, 3rd May 1882, at Amsterdam; with Colnaghi's; Mrs B. K. Young; with Spink and Son.

NOTES Although apparently authentically dated – no alteration can be seen – it is difficult for stylistic reasons, and impossible on account of the costume, to accept a date as early as 1702.

John Tillotson, London

83 AN ANCIENT COUPLE
1730's   Plate 17

SIZE $12\frac{1}{4} \times 9$ in / 31.1 × 22.9 cm

MEDIUM Pencil.

SIGNED AND DATED *M. Laroon F.* in ink and *1705* in pencil, perhaps an addition.

PROVENANCE L. G. Duke.

EXHIBITION London, Chesterfield House, *Marlborough and the Reign of Queen Anne,* 1934 (505).

NOTES The signature has not quite the running character of Laroon's hand and may have been inked over. Style and costume here also suggest a date later than 1705.

Brinsley Ford, London

84 FATHER AND FIVE SONS
(Family Group)
Probably 1733   Plate 14

SIZE $8\frac{3}{4} \times 12\frac{1}{2}$ in / 22.2 × 31.8 cm

MEDIUM Pencil.

INSCRIBED *Father & five Sons. eldest artist. 2 in ye army two at Sea.* and in another hand: *Capt Leroon.*

PROVENANCE Sir Edward Marsh; with the Squire Gallery in 1948; Gilbert Davis.

EXHIBITION London, Whitechapel Art Gallery, Spring 1906 (12).

NOTES From left to right are a military-looking young man leaning on the back of his father's chair who is sitting beside a small table; next to him is seated a son with dividers and another with a globe is leaning on the table. On the right is the artist holding a small painting and behind him the fifth son. This drawing has been called *The Laroon Family.* It cannot represent Lauron and his children as it is many years too late and he had only three sons; nor Marcellus who never married. It is unlikely to be John (see pp43–4) and nothing is known about James.

84 FATHER AND FIVE SONS
(Family Group) *continued*

Henry E. Huntington Library and
Art Gallery, San Marino, California

From stylistic affinities to the two dated groups of 1732/3 (48), (49) and from costume it can be dated about 1730. Possibly it is the sketch for the group referred to by Vertue in 1733 (*Vertue*, III, p64) 'he has lately painted a very large family peice valud at several hundred pounds' (see p51).

85 MUSIC PARTY (Vb)
1736   Plate 25

British Museum, London
Department of Prints and Drawings
(1959–7–11–2)

SIZE $9\frac{5}{8} \times 7\frac{13}{16}$ in / 24.4 × 20.2 cm

MEDIUM Pencil.

PROVENANCE Hubert Peake; Christie's, 17th March 1959 (16); with Colnaghi's from whom purchased by the Museum.

NOTES This is the undated sketch, with only minor differences, for (55). It is unfortunately not inscribed by Laroon.

86 MUSIC PARTY (VI)
1730's

Fig 65

Douglas H. Gordon,
Baltimore, Maryland

SIZE $8\frac{3}{4} \times 7$ in / 22.6 × 18.3 cm

MEDIUM Pencil.

PROVENANCE Christie's, 17th March 1959 (17); with Colnaghi's in 1959 from whom acquired by the present owner.

NOTES This is a preliminary sketch for the engraving, *M:L:Delin: Cl:DuBosc, Sculp:*, $14\frac{3}{8}$ by $19\frac{1}{8}$ in. 36.5 by 25.7 cm. captioned:

> *That Concert must each Passion move*
> *Whose Notes are all inspir'd by Love.*

There are numerous alterations in the engraving, notably in the 'cellist and the standing man on the right. The Laroon faces have become Du Bosc faces. As the drawing is not reversed it was probably not intended for engraving.

87 LADY WITH A FAN
1730's

Fig 66
Cyril Fry, London

SIZE $5\frac{7}{8} \times 4\frac{1}{4}$ in / 14.9 × 10.8 cm

MEDIUM Pencil.

88 TWO BOYS
1730's   Plate 28

Mr & Mrs Paul Mellon,
Upperville, Virginia

SIZE $10\frac{1}{2} \times 7\frac{3}{4}$ in / 26.7 × 19.7 cm

MEDIUM Pencil.

INSCRIBED *Design for ye Picture*, (in the upper margin) *Marcellus and John Lauron* or *Laroon, sons of Old Lauron or Laroon.* (in the lower margin) The inscriptions are in black ink and the lower one is over pencil – neither, apparently, in Laroon's hand.

PROVENANCE John Lane of the Bodley Head; Sotheby's, 30th June 1925 (114) as *Portrait Group of Marcellus and John Laroon*; Sir Robert Witt; with Colnaghi's, 1944; Iolo A. Williams.

NOTES This puzzling drawing is of Laroon's middle period. The design and figures are reminiscent of Lely. A possible but perhaps unlikely explanation is that it is a sketch of a painting from the Lely studio and that the upper inscription should read 'Design from ye Picture'. Only in this or some similar way could it represent the Laroon brothers.

89 OLD WOMAN TEACHING A BOY
1730's

Fig 67
Ashmolean Museum, Oxford

SIZE 10 × 7⅞ in / 25.4 × 20.0 cm

MEDIUM Pencil.

NOTES On the window ledge is a false signature *M. Laroon Fecit* and at the left lower corner *Captn. Larroon*.

90 BOY WITH A DOG
1730's

Fig 68
British Museum, London
Department of Prints and Drawings

SIZE 6$\frac{7}{16}$ × 5¼ in / 16.3 × 13.4 cm

MEDIUM Pencil.

NOTES This small drawing of a seated boy with a dog on his knee is stained and damaged.

91 A BIRDCATCHER
1730's   Plate 27

Dr R. E. Hemphill,
Barrow Gurney, nr. Bristol

SIZE 12⅛ × 7¾ in / 30.8 × 19.7 cm

MEDIUM Pencil and red chalk.

PROVENANCE With Colnaghi's in 1947 from whom bought by the present owner.

**92 MAN AND WOMAN
WITH A BAG OF GAME**
1730's   Plate 29

L. G. Duke, London

SIZE 8 × 11⅞ in / 20.3 × 30.1 cm

MEDIUM Pen and ink over pencil with watercolour.

PROVENANCE With Colnaghi's, 1957, from whom bought by the present owner.

NOTES A man in informal dress wearing spatterdashes hands a dead bird to a woman also informally dressed. By his feet lies an outsize dead hare. The bright blue and pinkish-red watercolour may be a later addition by another hand.

**93 NIGHT WALKERS
BEFORE A JUSTICE**
1740   Fig 36

With the Sabin Galleries, London

SIZE 7⅜ × 9⅜ in / 18.7 × 23.8 cm

MEDIUM Pencil and brown ink.

INSCRIBED *Night walkers brought before a Justice of ye peace* and on the verso in another hand, said to be that of the previous owner, Dorothy Richardson, *An original Sketch by Bunbury given to me by Mrs Bernard.*

PROVENANCE Mrs Bernard; Miss Dorothy Richardson (1748–1819) of Gargrave, Yorkshire; George Rondell Greene by family descent from the previous owner; Sotheby's, 7th July 1965 (32), as 'W. Hogarth'. It is possible but unlikely that this was the drawing in Samuel Scott's sale (see no. 56).

NOTES This is a preliminary and smaller version of the drawing at Windsor Castle *A Frenchman at Bow Street* (56).

**94 WEDDING NIGHT
(Throwing the Stocking)**
1740   Plate 32

SIZE 13 × 19⅜ in / 33 × 49.4 cm

MEDIUM Pencil.

PROVENANCE Dr John Percy (purchased from Parker), Percy Catalogue, p52–3, no. 1. 'Percy catalogue' in this and (97) and (112) refers to his MS catalogue of his drawings interleaved in a copy of the Burlington Fine Arts Club Catalogue of 1871 now in the Print Room of the British Museum; Percy sale, Christie's 17th April 1890 (737); Robert Low; Mrs Robert Low, who presented it to the Museum in 1910.

EXHIBITION London, British Museum, *William Hogarth*, 1964 (53).

94 WEDDING NIGHT
(Throwing the Stocking) *continued*
British Museum, London
Department of Prints and Drawings
(1910–2–18–44)

NOTES A complex scene, with more than forty figures, showing the traditional wedding night ceremony of throwing the stocking.

According to a former owner, Dr John Percy, an inscription by the artist on the old mount (now destroyed) read *Marcellus Laroon Fe 1740*.

95 A CONVERSATION
1740's   Plate 42

SIZE $15\frac{3}{8} \times 11\frac{1}{4}$ in / 39×28.7 cm

MEDIUM Pencil, pen and grey wash.

SIGNED *M. Laroon. F.*

LITERATURE A. P. Oppé, *English Drawings, Stuart and Georgian Periods, at Windsor Castle* (1950), p71, no. 411.

HM The Queen, Windsor Castle,
(Windsor Inventory 13287)

NOTES The old woman is in traditional bawd's dress.

96 A MERRY SUPPER PARTY
1740's   Plate 46

SIZE $5\frac{5}{8} \times 7\frac{3}{4}$ in / 14.3×19.7 cm

MEDIUM Pencil.

PROVENANCE A. P. Oppé.

Mr D.L.T. and Miss Armide Oppé,
London

NOTES The seven figures sitting round a primitive table include one who is clearly a bawd.

97 FASHIONABLE GROUP
WITH A DWARF
(Scene in the Mall)
1740's   Plate 43

SIZE $14\frac{3}{16} \times 9\frac{13}{16}$ in / 36.4×25.2 cm

MEDIUM Pen and ink over pencil with wash.

PROVENANCE Dr John Percy (purchased from Fawcett), Percy Catalogue, p52–3, no. 3 *Scene in the Mall*; Percy sale, Christie's, 17th April 1890 (736); L. G. Duke; H. B. Milling.

EXHIBITIONS Paris, Musée des Arts Décoratifs, *Caricatures et moeurs anglaises*, 1928 (67), as *The Dwarf*; London, Chesterfield House, *Marlborough and the Reign of Queen Anne*, 1934 (507).

Mrs W. W. Spooner, Ilkley

NOTES There is a faded inscription *by Laroon*.

98 HORSEMAN AND
BEGGAR
Probably 1760   Plate 57

SIZE $13\frac{1}{8} \times 9\frac{3}{4}$ in / 33.3×24.8 cm

MEDIUM Pencil.

98 HORSEMAN AND BEGGAR
continued

INSCRIBED *Capt: Marcellus Laroon (delt) 1730–*. The original pencil signature has been inked over by another hand, the *Capt* added and the *(delt)* altered probably from *fecit*. Stylistically the drawing is much later than 1730 and it is likely that the original date was 1760.

PROVENANCE Probably from the collection of the Mott family of The Hall, Barningham, Norfolk, as, when it came into Canon Parr's collection, it was in a scrapbook containing sketches mostly by members of the Mott family of the period 1823–33; Rev. Canon E. A. Parr, Norwich; Sotheby's, 14th November 1962 (57); with Colnaghi's 1962.

Mr & Mrs Paul Mellon,
Upperville, Virginia

EXHIBITION London, Blairman and Sons, *Marcellus Laroon*, 1951 (not in catalogue).

99 HORSEMAN AND HIS GROOM
Probably 1760's

Fig 69

Collection unknown

SIZE About $9\frac{1}{2} \times 7$ in / 24×18 cm

MEDIUM Pen and ink.

PROVENANCE Jhr. Alfr. Boreel, Amsterdam; in his sale at Amsterdam, 15th June 1908, as *Seigneur debout (un émigrant de Salzburg à Londres?) un garçon derrière lui tient son cheval*; sale of the collection of Mme V – –, Drouot, Paris, 30th March 1925, part 2 (89), as by *Learson*.

THREE ILLUSTRATIONS
100 The Quarrel Plate 63
101 The Duel Plate 64
102 Wounded Plate 65
Probably 1768

SIZE 100 $18\frac{1}{2} \times 12\frac{1}{2}$ in / 47.0×31.8 cm; 101 $19\frac{1}{4} \times 13\frac{1}{8}$ in / 48.9×33.3 cm
102 $19\frac{1}{2} \times 13\frac{1}{2}$ in / 49.5×34.3 cm

MEDIUM Reed pen with brown ink over pencil with wash.

SIGNED 100 *Marcellus. Laroon. F.*; 101 and 102 *Mar. Laroon. F.*

PROVENANCE 100 and 102 H. S. Reitlinger; Sotheby's, 27th January 1954 (170). 101 Sir Robert Witt; with Colnaghi's 1942, from whom bought by the Museum.

EXHIBITIONS 101 Paris, Musée des Arts Décoratifs, *Caricatures et moeurs anglaises*, 1928 (68).

NOTES These three drawings clearly belong to a narrative sequence. In the first a young man is running away from an older man who is about to draw his sword. A number of people watch, some from a window, one man from a wall, while a woman is about to intervene. In the second the two men are duelling with their seconds standing by. In the third the older man is being assisted to a chair by his second and another man. The other duellist on the right talks to his second. The rocky background is identical in 101 and 102.

Reitlinger, *Old Master Drawings*, 1922, p170, states that *The Quarrel*, which he entitles *Scene from a Comedy* is 'one of a series, one of which is dated 1768'. None of these drawings is dated and the one to which Reitlinger refers has not been found – but they certainly belong to the last few years of Laroon's life.

100 and 102 – Unknown collection
101 – British Museum – Department of Prints and Drawings
(1942–11–14–3)

103 A FIGHT
Probably 1770   Plate 68

SIZE 17¾ × 27¾ in / 45.1 × 70.5 cm

MEDIUM Reed pen and brown ink over pencil with wash.

PROVENANCE Francis Douce by whom bequeathed to the Ashmolean in 1834.

NOTES In a square of fine houses bands of waits are fighting with swords and with their musical instruments while the watch looks on helplessly.

The lower border has been cut but what is probably the top of the signature can be seen. The date is likely to be the same as that of the other two Douce drawings (64), (65) – 1770 – which it closely resembles.

Ashmolean Museum, Oxford

104 A FAMILY TEA PARTY
c 1770   Plate 69
(recto) and
THE EXECRABLE
CONCERT (verso)

SIZE 17 × 13¾ in / 43.3 × 33.8 cm

MEDIUM Reed pen and grey ink over pencil.

SIGNED *Mar. Laroon. F.*

PROVENANCE Sotheby's, 29th July 1931 (7a); Sotheby's, 4th November 1931 (6); L. G. Duke.

LITERATURE I. A. Williams, *The Listener*, 28th December 1932, p922.

EXHIBITIONS Paris, Musée des Arts Décoratifs, *Caricatures et moeurs anglaises*, 1928 (66); London, Royal Academy, *British Art*, 1934 (1116); Eton College, 1948 (2); London, Blairman and Sons, *Marcellus Laroon*, 1951 (E); London, Royal Academy, *Old Master Drawings*, 1953 (222); Washington, *English Drawings and Water Colors from the collection of Mr and Mrs Paul Mellon*, 1962 (44); Richmond, Virginia, *Painting in England 1700–1850. Collection of Mr and Mrs Paul Mellon*, 1963 (397).

NOTES On the upper third of the verso, occupying an area about 7 by 9 inches, is *The Execrable Concert*, reed pen and brown ink over pencil with wash. The title is Laroon's, and the drawing shows a fiddler, a man playing a one-stringed fiddle, two men making noises with a box (?) and fire-irons, and a man, who pulls the tails of cats imprisoned in a box to add to the din.

The size of the paper, the marginal pencil lines on the left and the sudden cutting-off on the right suggest that it may have been intended to be a large drawing of the size and something of the character of a high Wind (70).

Mr & Mrs Paul Mellon,
Upperville, Virginia

105 PIPE DRUNK
(Interior with two figures)
c 1770

Fig 70

University of London,
Courtauld Institute of Art
Witt Collection (2543)

SIZE $16\frac{1}{2} \times 12\frac{1}{2}$ in / 41.8×31.4 cm

MEDIUM Reed pen and ink over pencil with wash.

PROVENANCE Sir Robert Witt by whom bequeathed to the Courtauld Institute in 1952.

NOTES A man is emerging from some kind of a cubicle and a lighted pipe is passing between him and a fat woman seated at a small table. The meaning of this scene is difficult to define, but the subject is reminiscent of Dutch low-life scenes of tobacco dens.

106 HEAD OF AN OLD MAN
c 1770

Present owner not known

SIZE $4\frac{3}{4} \times 4\frac{7}{8}$ in / 11.0×12.4 cm

MEDIUM Reed pen and brown ink over pencil.

PROVENANCE C. Duits.

NOTES Head and shoulders of an old man wearing a three cornered hat with an ornament on top.

107 AN OLD MAN
c 1770

Fig 71

SIZE $12\frac{3}{8} \times 7\frac{1}{8}$ in / 32.7×18.1 cm

MEDIUM Reed pen and brown ink over pencil.

PROVENANCE Randall Davies; Davies sale, Sotheby's, 11th February 1947 (266), as *full length figure of a stout gentleman in a landscape*, sold with no. 80 in this catalogue; with Colnaghi's; Iolo A. Williams.

EXHIBITIONS Paris, Musée des Arts Décoratifs, *Caricatures et moeurs anglaises*, 1928 (65), as *Portrait of a Fat Man*.

NOTES From the head of the very fat old man with dropsy, this drawing appears to be of about 1770, but the rest of the figure has been heavily inked over probably by another hand.

Mr & Mrs Paul Mellon,
Upperville, Virginia

108	CONVERSATION IN AN OVAL	Sale of the Collection of James, Duke of Chandos, 8th May, 1747 (150). This might be the same as 21.

109	CONVERSATION	Lord Orford's Sale, 1753 (8).

110	A CONVERSATION OF LADIES AND GENTLEMAN	Sale of Pictures at The Green Door, date unknown (12). Probably a mid-Eighteenth Century sale. It is difficult to say whether 108, 109, and 110 are by Lauron or Laroon.

111	FIGURES MERRYMAKING	Lot 76 in the sale of Samuel Scott's collection on 13th January 1773. This may be one of the 'large drawings of merry makeings', which Vertue refers to in 1740, and which I have suggested were of the same kind as the Music Party drawings.

112	MOUNTEBANK	Lot 91 in the sale of Samuel Scott's collection on 13th January 1773, *A framed and glazed drawing of a Mountebank with a view of Covent Garden*. Possibly this was by Lauron, lot 3 in the Van Spangen sale, 1742/3, being *A Mountebank – Old Laroon*, not specified as drawing or painting.

113	SAVOYARDE IN THE YEAR 1697	Lot 75 in the Richard Bull sale at Sotheby's on 23rd May 1881, bought by Ellis; lot 16 in the van Huffel sale, Utrecht, 21st–23rd March 1933, described as pen and black chalk, 18 by 15 cm, signed, bought by Hofstede de Groot, but not now in the Hofstede de Groot Collection in the Museum van Oudheden, Groningen.

114	Mr MAVIS DRUNK	Lot 74 in the Richard Bull sale at Sotheby's, 23rd May 1881, *Mr. Mavis Drwck (sic) Study from Nature, in pencil, exceedingly clever*, bought by Ellis; in the sale of drawings of W. Pitcairn Knowles, at Amsterdam, 16th May 1899, *Laroon (M); Terborch (G), Mr. Mavis drunk; portrait d'homme assis. (Coll Landseer), Deux dessins, au crayon noir.*

115	GROUP OF HEADS	Dr John Percy (purchased from Pocock), Percy catalogue, p52–3, no. 2 'Indian Ink. 7.7 in (nearly) × 8.1 in (nearly)'; Percy Sale, Christie's, 17th April 1890 (736) with *Scene in the Mall* (Cat no 97).

116	LOVERS IN A GLADE IV (Jeune homme dans un bois)	Lot 137 in the sale of drawings of J. B. Heseltine, at Amsterdam, 27th May 1913, *jeune homme dans un bois déclarant son amour à une dame qui parait peu accessible à ses propositions*, pencil, 26.5 by 22.7 cm. Compare with nos. 2, 25, 29, and 61.

117	A MAN WITH A FEATHERED CAP	Lot 337 in the J. A. Jonkman sale at Amsterdam, 25th June 1929, *Un homme marchant vers la gauche; il porte un béret à plumes dans la main droite – plume au lavis de sanguine, 13.5 × 10.3 cm, Signé.*

| 118 | OLD WOMAN | Lot 495 in the F. van der Dussen sale at the Hague, 26th–28th June 1940, bought by Hofstede de Grote, but not now in the Hofstede de Groot Collection in the Museum van Oudheden, Groningen. Possibly the same as a drawing of an old woman at one time in the collection of John Bryson, Oxford. |

| 119 | FAMILY PIECE | 'he has lately painted a very large family peice valud at several hundred pounds'. *Vertue, III*, p64, 1733. See also no. 84. |

| 120 | OWEN MACSWINEY and others | 'Captain Laron. did some portraits from the life well painted a bold free manner. with good Spirit. his own picture Mr. Swineys. and others as big as the life.' *Vertue, III*, p100. See also no. 11. |

| 121 | JAMES DEACON (Senr.) | Seen by J. T. Smith at James Deacon's (Junr) who, he says, 'had a remarkably fine portrait in oils of his father, painted by Captain Laroon'. Smith, *Nollekens*, 1920 ed. vol. II, p204. |

| 122 | A SCREEN | According to Smith (*ibid.* p203) there were 'the remains of a curiously-gilt folding-screen in the great room of Hornsey-Wood House, most beautifully painted by Captain Laroon; upon which two of the figures are particularly spirited and full of broad humour, and represent a Quack Doctor and his Merry-Andrew, claiming the attention of, and amusing, the surrounding gaping and credulous spectators'. This screen, without mention of Laroon, is more fully described by William Hone in *Every-day Book*, pp760–1 '. . . a fine leather folding-screen. It still bears some remains of a spirited painting, spread over its leaves, to represent the amusements and humours of a fair in the low countries. At the top of a pole, which may have been the village May-pole, is a monkey with a cat on his back; then a sturdy bear-ward, in scarlet, with a wooden leg, exhibiting his bruin; an old woman telling fortunes to the rustics; a showman's drummer on the stage before a booth, beating up for spectators to the performance within, which the show-cloth represents to be a dancer on the tight-rope; a well set-out stall of toys, with a woman displaying their attractions; besides other interesting "bits" of a crowded scene, depicted by no mean hand, especially a group coming from a church in the distance, apparently a wedding procession the females well-looking and well dressed, bearing ribbons or scarfs below their waists in festoons'. |

| 123 | MOLL KING'S | 'I have seen at Strawberry-hill, a large and spirited drawing in red chalk, by Captain Laroon, exhibiting the inside of Moll King's. Kirgate, Mr. Walpole's domestic printer, bought it for him at an evening auction about forty years ago.' Smith, *ibid.* p190. |

Addenda

Nos 124 and 125 have been brought to my notice since the catalogue was in proof, the first through the kindness of Mr Keith K. Andrews of the National Gallery of Scotland and the second through that of Mr P. W. Ward-Jackson of the Victoria and Albert Museum.

124 BURIAL OF ROSAMOND

National Gallery of Scotland (on long loan from the Royal Scottish Academy)

SIZE 10 3/16 × 7 1/8 in/25.9 × 18.2 cm

MEDIUM Black and brown ink over black chalk with grey wash

SIGNED AND DATED *Mar. Laroon. F: 1746.*

INSCRIBED *The Burial of Rosamond. to be painted on a cloth of four foot* (erasure of measurements) *by three foot seven inches and a half*

PROVENANCE Probably in the collection of David Laing which was bequeathed to the Royal Scottish Academy in 1879; Royal Scottish Academy.

NOTES In the old ballads 'Fair Rosamond', after being poisoned by Queen Eleanor, is buried at either Woodstock or Godstow. Addison, in his opera *Rosamond* (1706/7) has the Queen tell the King, in Act III, Scene III, that

> The bowl, with drowsie juices fill'd
> From cold Egyptian drugs distill'd,
> In borrow'd death has clos'd her eyes:
> But soon the waking nymph shall rise,
> And in a convent plac'd, admire
> The cloister'd walls and virgin choire:

From the disarrangement of the shroud and the astonishment shown by the figures on the left it appears that Laroon is depicting the moment of Rosamond's awakening. A scene of this kind although not in Addison's libretto might easily have been interpolated to add dramatic interest to this tame and unsuccessful opera, possibly when it was reset by Arne in 1733. Or it may be another example of Laroon's use of the theatre as a starting point for an imaginary composition.
The exact (corrected) measurements imply that the painting was intended for some particular position.

125 WALPOLE-SCOTT CLUB

Tracing, in the collection of Mrs G. F. H. Bligh, London, by John Thomas Smith from Laroon's original drawing. See p90.
The original drawing is missing but the tracing (ink on tracing paper, 10 7/8 × 14 5/8 in/ 27.6 × 37.1 cm) can with confidence be equated with the tracing which John Thomas Smith made of Laroon's 'most beautiful drawing of the Members of this club in conversation, – – – when it was in the possession of my late worthy friend James Deacon' (Smith, *Nollekens and his Times*, 1829, Whitten's edition, 1920, pp 203–4). It is the kind of drawing which Laroon was making in the early thirties and the size is

Fig. 72

comparable (e.g. Cat. 48-51). Allowing for the inevitable loss of quality and individuality of draughtsmanship in the tracing it is not difficult to envisage the original.

Below the tracing is a cutting from John Green's *Odds and Ends about Covent Garden* with the figures identified by numbers. The figure of Laroon himself (3) is convincing, closely resembling the *Self Portrait* (Fig 14). The youthful Edward Walpole (1) born in 1706 – looks much as one might expect from later portraits and supports the dating of the drawing to the early thirties soon after his return from abroad in March 1730/31. Mr Kenneth Sharpe tells me that Mrs Scott's (7) is a more convincing likeness than that of her husband (6). 'Mr Mann' (4) is said by Green to be Robert Mann (d.1754) of the Customs House but the figure here appears to be too young and is not unlike the later portrait of Horace Mann (whose name is written on the tracing) painted by John Astley in 1751 (reproduced in W. S. Lewis, *Horace Walpole*, 1961, plate 18). If this identification is correct then it provides a terminal date for the drawing as Mann went to Florence in 1737. The portraits of James Deacon (5) who died in 1750 and of Bendall Martyn (2) are, I believe, unique. The James Deacon who owned Laroon's drawing when Smith traced it, would be the son of the Deacon shown here.

I had assumed as Laroon, Walpole, Deacon and Martyn were able and enthusiastic musicians that the *raison d'être* of the club was music but there is no suggestion of any musical activity here.

List of Collections (The numbers refer to the catalogue)

PUBLIC COLLECTIONS

Ashmolean Museum, Oxford: 64, 65, 89, 103; Birmingham City Museum and Art Gallery: 54; British Museum: 39, 47, 55, 58, 60, 81, 90, 94, 101; City Art Gallery, York: 20; Courtauld Institute of Art, University of London: 37, 48, 53, 68, 70, 80, 105; Fitzwilliam Art Gallery, Manchester: 50; National Gallery of Scotland: 41, 43; Tate Gallery, London: 22, 69; Whitworth Art Gallery, Manchester: 46; Henry E. Huntington Library and Art Gallery, San Marino, California: 51, 66, 84.

PRIVATE COLLECTIONS

Her Majesty The Queen: 1, 4, 52, 56, 95; H.R.H. The Princess Marina: 10; Professor I. R. C. Batchelor: 77; Michael Bevan Esq.: 5, 7, 23, 35, 78; The Duke of Buccleuch & Queensberry: 27; John Bryson Esq.: 49; M. Henri-Philippe Crombe: 8; L. G. Duke Esq., C.B.E.: 42, 76, 92; John Ehrman Esq.: 63; Brinsley Ford Esq.: 83; Cyril Fry Esq.: 87; Douglas H. Gordon Esq.: 86; Dr R. E. Hemphill: 91; Lady Martin: 28; Mr and Mrs Paul Mellon: 6, 11, 15, 16, 19, 25, 59, 73, 74, 75, 88, 98, 104, 107; Lord Methuen: 79; Sir Mordaunt Milner, Bart., S.A.: 33; Edmund Naylor Esq.: 24; D. L. T. Oppé Esq., and Miss Armide Oppé: 96; John Richardson Esq.: 38; Mr Seymour Slive: 62; Mrs W. W. Spooner: 97; Basil Taylor Esq.: 61; John Tillotson Esq.: 82; H. C. Torbock Esq.: 67; Miss G. M. Trumper: 34; Paul Walraf Esq.: 44; Samuel Whitbread Esq.: 13; Eric Wood Esq.: 21; Anon. collections: 3, 9, 12, 18, 26, 30, 31, 72; Collections unknown: 2, 17, 40, 45, 71, 99, 100, 102, 106.

Plates

Plate 1 *Grotesque Musicians* c 1700
8 11/16 × 12 3/4 ins L. G. Duke Cat. 76

Plate 2 *Broken on the Wheel* c 1710
11 1/8 × 8 5/8 ins I. R. C. Batchelor Cat. 77

Plate 3 *A Musical Assembly* 1715–20 40 × 50 ins
HRH Princess Marina Cat. 10

Plate 3 Detail

Plate 4 *A Dinner Party* 1719 $11\frac{1}{2} \times 9\frac{7}{8}$ ins P. D. Matthiesen Cat. 40

Plate 5 *A Dinner Party* 1725 36 × 33⅞ ins Reproduced by gracious permission of HM The Queen Cat. 1

Plate 6 *Mat Ashton at Chester* Before 1725
$8\frac{3}{4} \times 12\frac{7}{8}$ ins University of London
Courtauld Institute Cat. 80

Plate 7 *Man holding a Book* 1724
$7\frac{5}{8} \times 6$ ins L. G. Duke Cat. 42

Plate 8 *A Lady and Gentleman at Tea* 1729
$12\frac{1}{8} \times 7\frac{7}{8}$ ins National Gallery of
Scotland Cat. 43

Plate 9 *A Gentleman in Green* c 1730 28 × 24⅝ ins Private collection Cat. 12

Plate 10 *Music Party* (*Ia*) 1731 14¾ × 12 ins Paul Walraf Cat. 44

Plate 11 *Group of Figures at a Table* (*I*)
1732/3 7½ × 9¾ ins University of London
Courtauld Institute Cat. 48

Plate 12 *Group of Figures at a Table* (*II*)
1732/3 7⅞ × 9¾ ins John Bryson Cat. 49

Plate 13 *A Farmer putting his Son apprentice to an Attorney* 1731 13⅛ × 18¾ ins Whitworth Art Gallery
Cat. 46

Plate 14 *Father and Five Sons* Prob. 1733
8¾ × 12½ ins Henry E. Huntington
Library & Art Gallery Cat. 84

Plate 15 *Scene in a Garden* 1732 16⅛ × 11 11/16 ins British Museum Cat. 47

Plate 16 *A Dutchman and his Wife* 1730s 15¼ × 11½ ins John Tillotson Cat. 82

Plate 17 *An Ancient Couple* 1730s 12¼ × 9 ins Brinsley Ford Cat. 83

Secretary to the Excise.

Plate 18 *Music Party (IIb)* 1733 10⅝ × 8¼ ins Henry E. Huntington Library & Art Gallery Cat. 51

Plate 19 *The Village Wedding* 1735 43 × 37½ ins Private collection, England Cat. 3

Plate 20 *Fête Galante* c 1735 36 × 28 ins (?) Destroyed in 1940 Cat. 14

Plate 21 *Riders and Beggars* 1735 18¼ × 13 ins Reproduced by gracious permission of
HM The Queen Cat. 52

Plate 22 *Music Party (III)* 1735 15½ × 11 ins University of London, Courtauld Institute Cat. 53

Plate 23 *Music Party (IV)* 1735 17¾ × 13 ins Birmingham City Museum Cat. 54

Plate 24 *Music Party* (*Va*) 1736 17⅞ × 13⅛ ins British Museum Cat. 55

Plate 25 *Music Party* (*Vb*) 1736 9⅝ × 7 13/16 ins British Museum Cat. 85

Plate 26 *Officer and Lady at Supper* c 1735 $14\frac{3}{8} \times 12\frac{1}{4}$ ins Mr & Mrs Paul Mellon Cat. 16

Plate 27 *A Birdcatcher* 1730s
12⅛ × 7¾ ins Dr R. E. Hemphill Cat. 91

Plate 28 *Two Boys* 1730s $10\frac{1}{2} \times 7\frac{3}{4}$ ins
Mr & Mrs Paul Mellon Cat. 88

Plate 29 *Man and Woman with a Bag of Game* 1730s $8 \times 11\frac{7}{8}$ ins
L. G. Duke Cat. 92

Plate 30 *A Musical Tea Party* 1740 36 × 28 ins Reproduced by gracious permission of HM The Queen Cat. 4

Plate 31 *A Frenchman at Bow Street* 1740 $14\frac{1}{8} \times 20\frac{1}{2}$ ins Reproduced by gracious permission of
HM The Queen Cat. 56

Plate 32 *Wedding Night* 1740 13 × 19⅜ ins British Museum Cat. 94

Plate 33 *The Black Prince* c1740 54 × 45½ ins Collection unknown Cat. 17

Plate 34 *Scene from Henry the Fourth, Part I* 1746 $35\frac{1}{2} \times 28\frac{1}{4}$ ins Mr & Mrs Paul Mellon Cat. 6

Plate 35 *Tavern Interior with Peasants* 1742 $18\frac{1}{2} \times 15\frac{1}{4}$ ins
Michael Bevan Cat. 5

Plate 36 *Stage Figure* c 1740 $24\frac{1}{2} \times 16\frac{3}{4}$ ins
Private collection, England Cat. 18

Plate 37 *Promenade in the Mall* 1744 15⅝ × 11⅞ ins British Museum Cat. 58

Plate 38 *Rocky Landscape with Figures*
1743 13½ × 10 15/16 ins University of
London, Courtauld Institute Cat. 57

Plate 39 *Figures Walking* 1744
16¾ × 13¼ ins Mr & Mrs Paul Mellon
Cat. 59

Plate 40 *The Woodman* 1748
$8\frac{7}{8} \times 6\frac{11}{16}$ ins British Museum Cat. 60

Plate 41 *The Woodman* 1748 $35\frac{1}{2} \times 27\frac{1}{2}$ ins Michael Bevan Cat. 7

Plate 42 *A Conversation* 1740s $15\frac{3}{8} \times 11\frac{1}{4}$ ins Reproduced by gracious permission of
HM The Queen Cat. 95

Plate 43 *Fashionable Group with a Dwarf* 1740s 14 $\frac{3}{16}$ × 9 $\frac{13}{16}$ ins Mrs W. W. Spooner Cat. 97

Plate 44 *The Rencontre* c 1750 36 × 24 ins City Art Gallery, York Cat. 20

Plate 45 *Interior with Figures* c 1750
17 × 15 ins Tate Gallery Cat. 22

Plate 46 *A Merry Supper Party* 1740s
5⅝ × 7¾ ins Mr D. L. T. and
Miss Armide Oppé Cat. 96

Plate 47 *A Gentleman in Brown* c 1750 34¼ × 27¾ ins Michael Bevan Cat. 23

Plate 48 *James Macardell* 175(?4) $23\frac{1}{2} \times 15\frac{3}{4}$ ins Henri-Phillipe Crombé Cat. 8

Plate 49 *Lady and Gentleman with a Page* c 1750–5 30 × 25 ins Edmund Naylor Cat. 24

Plate 50 *Lovers in a Glade (III)* 1759
$13\frac{3}{8} \times 10\frac{3}{16}$ ins Basil Taylor Cat. 61

Plate 51 *Lovers in a Glade (II)* c 1750–5 35 × 27 ins Mr & Mrs Paul Mellon Cat. 25

Plate 52 *The Card Players* 1760 25 × 21 ins Private collection, Beirut Cat. 9

Plate 53 *A Musical Conversation* (*I*) c 1760 27¼ × 35 ins Duke of Buccleuch Cat. 27

Plate 54 *A Musical Conversation* (*II*) c 1760 25½ × 30¼ ins Lady Martin Cat. 28

Plate 55 *Horseman and Fruitseller* c 1760 $20\frac{1}{2} \times 13$ ins Private collection, England Cat. 30

Plate 56 *Lady and Gentleman riding through a Wood* c 1760 21 × 12⅞ ins Private collection Cat. 31

Plate 57 *Horseman and Beggar*
Probably 1760 $13\frac{1}{8} \times 9\frac{3}{4}$ ins
Mr & Mrs Paul Mellon Cat. 98

Plate 58 *Horseman Stopping for Wine* c 1760 $18 \times 14\frac{3}{4}$ ins Sir Mordaunt Milner, Bt.
Cat. 33

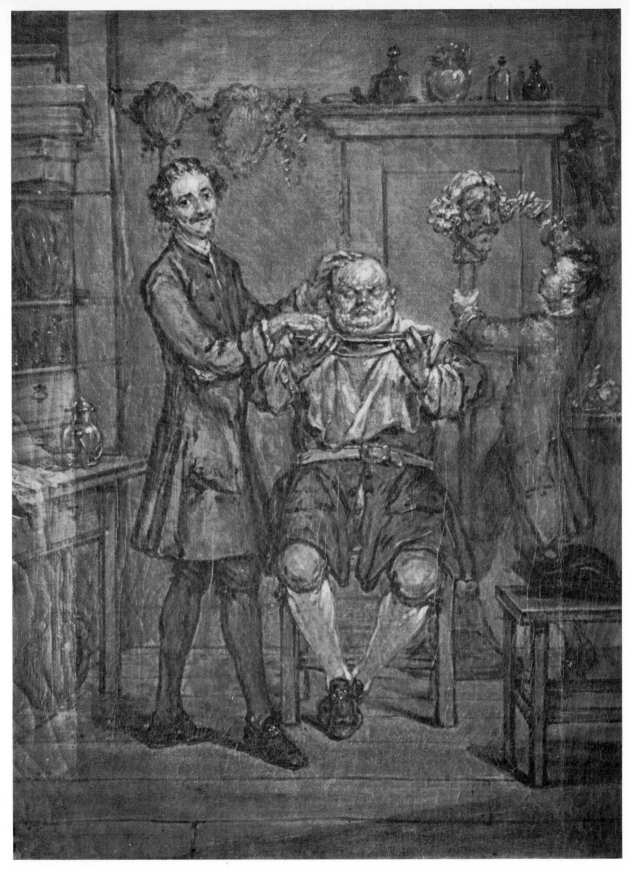

Plate 59 *The Barber's Shop* 1760s 17 × 13 ins Miss G. M. Trumper Cat. 34

Plate 60 *The Song* 1760 13⅛ × 10¼ ins Michael Bevan Cat. 35

Plate 61 *A German, A Frenchman* 1762
$9\frac{5}{8} \times 13$ ins Seymour Slive Cat. 62

Plate 62 *Young Man in a Tavern* 1760s
$14\frac{5}{16} \times 12\frac{1}{4}$ ins with M. Bernard Cat. 36

Plate 63 *The Quarrel* Probably 1768
$18\frac{1}{2} \times 12\frac{1}{2}$ ins Collection unknown Cat. 100

Plate 64 *The Duel* Probably 1768 $19\frac{1}{4} \times 13\frac{1}{8}$ ins
British Museum Cat. 101

Plate 65 *Wounded* Probably 1768 $19\frac{1}{2} \times 13\frac{1}{2}$ ins
Collection unknown Cat. 102

Plate 66 *Cudgeling* 1770 18⅜ × 27¾ ins Ashmolean Museum, Oxford Cat. 65

Charity.   Ætatis 92   Marcellus Laroon F. 1770.

Plate 67 *Charity* 1770 16 × 24½ ins Ashmolean Museum, Oxford Cat. 64

Plate 68 *A Fight* 1770 17¾ × 27¼ ins Ashmolean Museum, Oxford Cat. 103

Plate 69 *A Family Tea Party* c 1700
17 × 13¼ ins Mr & Mrs Paul Mellon
Cat. 104

Plate 70 *The Morning Ride* 1770
14 × 11 ins Henry E. Huntington
Library & Art Gallery Cat. 66

Plate 71   *A High Wind*   1771   20$\frac{11}{16}$ × 30$\frac{13}{16}$ ins   University of London, Courtauld Institute   Cat. 70

Plate 72 *Cavalrymen on the March* 1771
$18\frac{7}{8} \times 12\frac{3}{4}$ ins University of London
Courtauld Institute Cat. 68

Plate 73 *A Hunting Party* 1771 $19\frac{1}{4} \times 13$ ins
Tate Gallery Cat. 69

Plate 74 *Street Scene* 1772 $18\frac{3}{4} \times 12\frac{1}{2}$ ins
Private collection, England Cat. 72

Index

Numbers in bold type (**2**) refer to the figures and plates.
Numbers expressed as '**F2**' refer to illustrations in the main text, and in the catalogue.
Numbers expressed as '**P2**' refer to illustrations in the section of plates beginning
on page 155.
All titles of pictures and literary works are given in italics.
An asterisk following a name (e.g. Millar, Oliver cit.*) indicates that
the author's publication(s) is/are listed in the Bibliography on pp. 103-6.